WORKPLACE CULTURE & THE NDIS

WORKPLACE
CULTURE
& THE NDIS

A Guide
for Leaders
in the Australian
Disability Sector

FRAN CONNELLEY

'Your book resonates so well with the reality of the NDIS experience. It is current, recent and such a good synopsis of the new marketplace and the issues we face. I've gifted copies to every board member and every one on my senior leadership team. Keep up the fantastic work!'

Caroline Cuddihy, Chief Executive Officer, Sunnyfield disAbility Services

'This book, and Fran's key messages, really get to the heart of what the NDIS was originally envisaged to accomplish. As Chair of a disability service provider, parent of a child with a lifetime disability, and as a professional working in the non-profit space, I gained enormous practical insights that I will take with me to board meetings, strategy sessions and advocacy discussions.'

Robert Crowe, Leading For Purpose

'A great read and a fabulous resource. Thanks Fran.'

Suzanne Hicks, Director at Newcastle Consulting and Counselling Services

'Fran has captured what organisations need in their workplace to improve the culture within their business. She is excellent at identifying the fundamentals required for an organisation's success within the disability sector. Congratulations on yet another successful book and tool.'

René Viljoen, Regional Coordinator – WA|Perth, Peel, Wheatbelt & Esperance Regions – Ernst & Young Consulting Services – BLCW Program

'People need to be re-inspired, re-nourished and re-calibrated in order to maintain a quality service. As Stephen Covey says: "To keep the main thing the main thing is the main thing." And that's what your work does. Thank you for all the work you are doing.'

Martin Porteous, Joint CEO, Inala

'"Lead with Vision, Purpose and Integrity." This quote says so much about the tone of this great book. A must read for those operating in the disability sector to get the most from your workforce and to give the most to your clients.'

Clare Malcolm, Disability Workforce Innovation Connector, National Disability Services

'The most important thing I found was the absolute value of the client and how important they are to the whole organisation. Your book makes it all personal and we all need to own the "brand". Thank you.'

Kerry Strange, Manager, Art Central

'Fran Connelley has challenged the disability industry to think differently about our customers and position them in the centre of everything we do. She has given our organisation the confidence to stick to our guns during a time when glossy rebrands were the norm and focus on supporting our staff through one of the biggest culture change processes of our organisation's history. If Fran says it, do it.'

Jess Brown, Group Manager, Business Growth, Marathon Health

'As CEO of Westhaven, Fran worked with us to develop a well-defined Strategic Marketing Plan. The process she guided us through, and documented for us, created a clear road map for our charity's future under NDIS. Fran is an insightful and passionate advocate for the work that NGOs do that makes so many disadvantaged people's lives better. I'd welcome the opportunity to work with her again as she is dedicated to clarity of purpose and prioritising the markets that NGOs work within to build a sustainable business model.'

Christian Grieves, former CEO, Westhaven Association

'Fran is the real deal when it comes to bringing marketing strategy to life and really understands that critical connection between supporting a vibrant, high-performing workplace culture and the strength of your organisation's brand.'

Edward Birt, Chief Operating Officer, The Disability Trust

'For not-for-profit organisations operating in the competitive NDIS market-place, the reality is that recruiting staff and attracting clients to our services are equally important challenges. Fran brings deep insights and a marketer's perspective to this challenge in a way that stimulates thinking and action but is at the same time accessible and always focused on the most important thing: the people we are here to help and our organisational mission and values.'

Birgitte Maibom, Chief Executive Officer, Learning Links

'Authentic and knowledgeable – that's exactly how I would describe Fran. Her passion for seeing organisations perform at their optimum is reflected throughout her books and her speaking engagements. As an NDIS and disability expert, Fran excels in sharing compelling, realistic and unique stories of triumph and inspiration. She has a natural ability to connect emotionally and effectively to motivate and inspire both a community and corporate audience. She understands the external policy and social landscape and can subsequently tailor her communication style to a diverse audience. I have learnt much from her – she is a rare gem.'

Simone Power, Engagement & Partnerships Manager, Cerebral Palsy Support Network

'Fran's Culture Masterclass was one of the best workshops I've ever attended and one that I will measure all future workshops against. Loved it! The activities were fabulous! 10/10.'

Mandy Zankar, HR Director, Vivid Vic

'When Allevia was facing the daunting challenge of transitioning over to the NDIS, Fran was a key to us unlocking our vision, giving clarity to our true mission, and agreement on the values and behaviours we accept as being the core of the Allevia Way. Fran challenged us to look deeply at our impact on the community and the people we serve and to redefine ourselves in an emerging market. The work we did with Fran has changed our view of ourselves and assisted us to shape a workplace culture which is grounded in clear organisation-wide values that drive everyone's behaviours.'

Philip Petrie, CEO, Allevia

'Your process has delivered a miracle.'

Helen Jeffs, Executive Manager Business Development, Marathon Health

'Fran's marketing expertise combined with the design and delivery of her strategic marketing program has provided the opportunity for much-needed organisational change.'

Greg Kerr, Director, Illawarra Multicultural Services

Dedicated to my wonderful father, Frank Stackpool, who taught me to always question anything I couldn't understand.

We lost you way too soon.

'Culture eats strategy for breakfast.'

Peter Drucker

'Your employees have to love your organisation
before your customer ever will.'

Simon Sinek

'Organisational culture is the accumulated learning of the group that
is a pattern of system of beliefs, values and behavioural norms that
come to be taken for granted as basic assumptions and eventually
drop out of awareness.'

Edgar Schein, PhD Professor Emeritus, MIT Sloan School of Management

Author's note

I am indebted to the hundreds of people who bought my first book and then came back and bought extra copies for their board and staff. For a first time self-publishing author, the success of *How to Thrive Under the NDIS* surprised me more than anyone else.

Over the last three years I've come to realise that the National Disability Insurance Scheme is not one animal. Its shape changes in every state and every region. So, attempting to write a book about it once again feels like a risky business.

The NDIA Price Guide is still the single greatest threat to the supply of quality services in this sector, as evidenced in several Productivity Commission reports. However, in recent months, pricing has begun to head in the right direction. The combined impact of the March 2019 price increases and the indexed increase is approximately 20% to 27%.

To date, the predicted new market entrants have been largely confined to online businesses and sole traders as the controlled pricing offered little incentive for other business models.

As a result, we now have a market where demand greatly exceeds the sector's capacity to supply and one of the greatest challenges for providers is workforce.

In this second book I have tried to focus on the area where I feel I can most add value, by offering a marketer's approach to workforce culture.

Despite the rhetoric, the NDIS is not Medicare. The disability customer is not looking to make a transaction. They are looking for quality services from someone they can trust. As a result, more than ever before, the frontline, customer-facing staff member is now the service provider's most important asset. If they feel heard, valued and supported, so will the customer.

This goes directly to the culture of an organisation. In the perfect storm of the NDIS it is culture that holds organisations together and cultural fatigue that splits them into silos.

I should say up front that this book does not cover quantitative measurement or staff engagement surveys as there are solutions available that already address this area. Nor does it get into the operational issues of workforce management.

I'd like to thank the interviewees. They generously donated their time, ideas and practical frontline learnings in the hope that their experience would help build sector capacity. I am indebted to each of them.

Finally, I'd like to address the terminology. Throughout this book I use the terms 'customers' and 'participants' interchangeably. 'Participants' is the descriptor for people who receive NDIS funding.

I also use the term 'non-profit'. For many reasons the term 'non-profit' is unhelpful and 'for-purpose' may be preferable. However, some of the most successful 'for-profit' organisations are clearly purpose driven. All 'non-profits' must earn and retain some profit in order to keep their doors open, hire quality staff and deliver quality services for the communities they serve. So the term 'non-profit' is plagued with issues. However, after much to-ing and fro-ing I have used it, with apologies in advance to anyone whom it offends.

Thank you for reading this book.

About the author

Fran Connelley is a strategic marketer, author, facilitator and presenter specialising in the non-profit sector. Over the last 20 years, as Director of FC Marketing, she has helped many well-known organisations build their brands, clarify their message, share their stories and diversify their revenue. Fran first began working with disability organisations in 2008 and is currently working with organisations in NSW, South Australia, Queensland and Victoria.

She is passionate about using marketing principles to improve the employee experience. Her latest workshops, *Bringing the Brand Alive* and *The Culture Masterclass*, help leaders re-energise their workplace culture in the face of the NDIS. A compulsive learner, Fran is inspired by Frederic Laloux, Simon Sinek, Peter Drucker, Seth Godin, Aaron Dignan, L. David Marquet, Stephen Covey, Malcolm Gladwell, Michael E. Gerber and Eric Reis.

Her first book, *How to Thrive Under the NDIS: A pathway to sustainability for service providers*, is now in its seventh reprint. It's available from Amazon, Booktopia and direct from www.fcmarketing.com.au.

First published in 2020 by Fran Connelley

Reprinted February 2020

A catalogue entry for this book is available from the National Library of Australia.

ISBN: 978-1-925921-40-3

Project management and text design by Michael Hanrahan Publishing
Cover design by Peter Reardon

Disclaimer
The material in this publication is of the nature of general comment only, and does not represent professional advice. It is not intended to provide specific guidance for particular circumstances and it should not be relied on as the basis for any decision to take action or not take action on any matter which it covers. Readers should obtain professional advice where appropriate, before making any such decision. To the maximum extent permitted by law, the author and publisher disclaim all responsibility and liability to any person, arising directly or indirectly from any person taking or not taking action based on the information in this publication.

Contents

Foreword

Professor David J. Gilchrist[1]

The National Disability Insurance Scheme (NDIS) is complex and challenging but very important. Indeed, its importance cannot be understated as it has the potential to positively impact the lives of millions of Australians living with disability, and to drive social and economic improvement nationally – changing the lives of many more people for the better.

In terms of the delivery of services and supports to those people living with disability, the aspirations of the NDIS are, amongst other things, to deliver greater choice and control to those people who participate as service users in order to give them a real say in what supports they receive, when and by whom those supports are given. This is an aspect of the NDIS that has gathered so much support across the Australian community.

To facilitate this process, the NDIS funding arrangements have been developed so that they are akin to a marketplace that is intended to facilitate the decision making needed to deliver control to the client.

---

1   Professor David J. Gilchrist is an economic historian and chartered accountant. He currently holds a chair in accounting at the University of Western Australia, researches in the area of human services delivery and public policy, and is co-convenor of Not-for-profits UWA at that institution.

Generally, before the advent of the NDIS, the primary funding stakeholder was the state or territory government. It provided funding for disability services and it also established the key attributes of service delivery (or business rules) including in relation to the important questions of: (1) what should be delivered; (2) how much should be delivered; (3) when should it be delivered; and (4) by whom should it be delivered.

The NDIS is intended to 'correct' the locus of control and to widen the opportunities for people living with disability so that clients are more likely to achieve better outcomes. As such, the NDIS 'market style' of funding also impacts the service providers because, arguably, their primary stakeholder is the client because choice and control means that clients are intended to have control over the funding allocation.

This is not to say that prior to the NDIS, disability service providers were uninterested in their clients. However, it does mean that different people are potentially making different decisions about what services they want, particularly in the case of decision making within an organisation. This, in turn, impacts the service providers who now need to respond to individual client requirements rather than a funder's requirements. Staff who are closer to clients (including their carers) need to be making decisions and responding to client needs directly while the bureaucratic potential needs to be reduced as much as possible.

Because this former funding arrangement was in place for a number of decades in most jurisdictions, disability service providers – whether Not-for-profit or For-profit – became fit-for-purpose under this policy framework over long years of operating within a set government policy. Now, with the NDIS rolling out across Australia and itself being a new policy framework in which providers must operate, these organisations have to rethink their structures, resourcing and strategies in order to be fit-for-purpose under the new arrangements, which also means they need to undertake activities (such as those addressed in this book) which they did not necessarily need to consider before.

Importantly, and as so eloquently put by Fran Connelley in this volume, the change in funding arrangements, combined with the universally accepted aspiration of choice and control, means that disability service providers need to ensure that their clients trust them, understand them and that they can respond positively to meet their needs effectively. To achieve this outcome, service providers will rely heavily on their frontline staff who are the first to engage with potential and current clients, who represent the organisation and who need to be developed to represent its ethos and authenticity positively. Without such investment, disability service providers face the risk of becoming remote from their clients and leaving them with a desire to look elsewhere for their supports.

This, Fran Connelley's latest book, articulates clearly the need for organisations involved in the disability services sector to take the issue of staff development seriously and describes practical methods designed to assist leaders in the disability services sector to achieve positive change at the service level of their organisation. It is based on Fran's considerable practical knowledge and industry experience, ensuring it is both insightful and practical.

The resources at the command of these organisations are generally small and Fran's expertise and experience in managing in this environment adds considerable value to the reader, allowing them to use this resource at the coalface of day-to-day organisational development. She uses a wide variety of examples to support her very practical recommendations.

I am delighted to see this volume published as the success of the NDIS – a success that we all hope for – is in part dependent on the reshaping of the disability services sector so that it is robust, efficient and so that it effectively responds to the needs of those people living with disability. Becoming fit-for-purpose under the new funding model will help to ensure the aspirations of the NDIS are realised.

It will also help to ensure that a national asset, the disability services sector, develops and responds to the challenges so that Australia retains its disability services capacity into the future.

Introduction

The sliding doors of meningitis

This is a story that I didn't include in my previous book. In fact, I didn't really share it anywhere until early last year. It initially tumbled out as I tried to explain to a friend *why* the disability sector feels like a personal mission for me. He told me to start sharing it – immediately.

The story begins with a chance encounter at a conference I attended in 2001. At the time I was working as a sponsorship marketing consultant for a large environmental organisation called Landcare Australia.

During one of the coffee breaks I noticed a woman standing to one side by the wall, sipping a cup of tea on her own. She seemed very flat, very alone. I can still see her. So I went up, introduced myself, and then after chatting for a little while I eventually managed to ask if she was okay.

She explained that her sister had died the week before, at the age of 42. (I remember thinking, *what a coincidence, that's my age*.) She went on to say that her sister 'hadn't led much of a life'. For the last 40 years she had been either in a wheelchair or a bed, living in the same institution, unable to feed herself and unable to speak, due to a severe intellectual disability caused by contracting bacterial meningitis at the age of two.

Bacterial meningitis is a swelling of the brain membrane and spinal cord. The initial symptoms appear like the flu and then, after only a few hours, the child may go stiff and scream at any movement. If it isn't diagnosed within two or three days the result is severe brain damage. If it isn't diagnosed within a week, it's fatal.

So why did this story mean so much to me? Why did it tear me apart and reassemble me?

Because I had also caught bacterial meningitis at the same age in the same 1960 outbreak in Sydney. (It's funny, but it's still hard to tell this story; it's even harder to read that last sentence.)

My dear mum knew something was wrong with me as I lay stiff in my bed, not wanting to be moved or touched. Just a few days earlier, I'd been a happy, healthy toddler on a family ferry trip from Circular Quay.

When dad returned home late from work that night, the story goes that he took one look at me, picked me up and took me straight into town, rushing me into casualty saying, 'I don't know what she's got but give her everything you have.'

And they did. Even today, huge early doses of antibiotics are the only effective treatment for bacterial meningitis.

I received immediate treatment only because I had the incredible good fortune to have a father who was a doctor at that time in the emergency department of the old Children's Hospital at Camperdown.

I always knew I was fortunate to have such wonderful, loving parents, but this 'good luck' hit an entirely new level for me that day at the conference. The questions that have stuck in my brain since that day have been, 'Why was I the lucky one? Why couldn't she have had the same luck?' And the big one: 'How is this fair?'

We were both 42. It hit us both 40 years earlier.

By then I'd raised a few million in cash and pro bono support for wetland rehabilitation, rainforests and coastal zone protection. But for the first time I recognised an undeniable truth: *here was my cause.* Disability became visceral for me.

Over the last year or so I've shared this story at every speaking event, and nearly every time someone in the audience tells me they have a sister or a brother who also contracted bacterial meningitis as a child and that they now have a severe intellectual disability. Every time I hear it I think, *that could have been me.*

Why we need the NDIS to work and new metrics to measure it

In 2008, Australia became one of the first countries to ratify the UN Convention on the Rights of Persons with Disabilities. Yet in terms of quality of life, Australia sits last in OECD rankings on poverty for people with disabilities.[2]

Recent data from the Australian Institute of Health and Welfare estimates that 4.3 million Australians live with a disability That's one in five people. Nearly 32% of those have severe or profound disability.[3]

The same report goes on to say that people with disability are four times more likely to experience psychological distress than other Australians, and also suffer poorer outcomes in areas such as physical health, education and employment.

In 2011, nearly 45% of people with disability lived on or near the poverty line.[4] That's nearly two million people. This would not be news for most of you reading this book, however it is the reason

---

2   PwC, 'Disability expectations – Investing in a better life, a stronger Australia', Canberra, 2011.

3   Australian Institute of Health and Welfare 2019. People with disability in Australia. Cat.no. DIS72. Canberra: AIHW https://www.aihw.gov.au/reports/disability/people-with-disability-in-Australia.

4   PwC, 'Disability expectations – Investing in a better life, a stronger Australia', Canberra, 2011.

we need a robust, fully functioning disability market and a National Disability Insurance Scheme that fulfils its promise.

Yet, far more important than numerical targets is the human cost if the NDIS doesn't work. We need to review our performance measures for this reform to make sure people's lives are actually being improved. It would be far more meaningful if the NDIA's (National Disability Insurance Agency) funding was not simply tied to the number of participants with NDIS Plans (how could this ever be used to measure choice and control?) but to the hard evidence of quality participant outcomes across an equitable spread of metro, rural and remote regions.

Why workplace culture? (aka: Jane spits the dummy)

Over the last four years, the Australian disability sector has experienced massive industry disruption due to the NDIS, which replaces traditional 'block' funding of organisations with individual funding 'packages' paid directly to the consumer or 'participant'.

Smart businesses are built on strong cultures. It's culture that enables people to perform at their best. In the rush and confusion created by the NDIS, the disability workforce is now experiencing change and cultural fatigue on an unprecedented scale.

It was December 2017 when it first hit me that I needed to shift my focus from marketing strategy to workforce culture. I was attending a disability industry conference in Sydney and chatting with a disability support worker at the break. She worked for a very new, very large non-profit provider of group home accommodation. (Let's call her Jane.)

As soon as I mentioned that I was a marketer Jane rolled her eyes, saying:

> **Look, marketing is all very well, but I was a public servant and I thought I had a job for life.**

**I know I shouldn't say this but I feel like I've
just been sold. I now work for a large NGO
and they're telling me I have to be a brand
ambassador. What the hell does that even *mean*?**

New South Wales was the first state to fully 'roll out'. With
that rollout came the sale of all state government–run group home
accommodation. Across NSW, there was a massive transfer of assets
and people. Here was an extremely capable, dedicated woman with
a new employer whom she didn't trust. Jane just wanted to be able
to do her job.

At the same conference, a CEO proudly told me that his organisation would grow from a revenue base of $6 million to $20 million – in the next three months! They were adding 460 new staff
and moving into new premises. (And this guy was smiling – go
figure …)

I started wondering, how many more frontline support workers (how many more Janes?) were feeling as frustrated and disillusioned? Are the leadership skills in this space really up for this scale
of challenge? What would be the impact on the already confused
NDIS participant?

It hit me then and there that the speed and scale of change I was
witnessing would impact quality at every level of the organisation –
and that, if I really wanted to make a difference, I needed to shift my
focus to workplace culture. Because in this sector the customer is
always going to feel what the employee feels.

The cultural challenges associated with that scale of change are
massive, particularly when you consider that organisations were
simultaneously reinventing their operations in order to adapt to the
new NDIS funding model.

In December 2017, solvency suddenly became the single hottest
issue for providers as they struggled to handle the volume of NDIS

Plan errors and implementation flaws while keeping their doors open. The personal and financial cost of dealing with the NDIA, the staff burnout, change fatigue, poor communications, poor transition plans, and loss of mission focus all contributed to a sector in shock.

'Whatever you do, don't mention marketing!'

Three months later in March 2018 I was invited to speak to 250 staff of a large disability service provider. The brief was initially simple: 'present an overview of the key challenges facing disability providers'. However, their marketing director added the comment, 'Whatever you do, *don't mention marketing.*' I pointed out that as a marketing consultant this might be a little tricky.

I'm relieved to say the presentation went down really well. In fact, it was a joy the way they responded. For the first time, I really dived into the role of workplace culture, the employee experience and the customer's experience – from a marketer's viewpoint.

I spoke about the role of the values-based internal brand in building a high-performance team culture. I talked about why some brands were incredibly strong and how they can unite teams in times of change. I talked about the synergy that happens when an individual feels that their own personal values are aligned with those of their employer. I talked about the organisation's most important asset being their staff. I talked about the stories we need to tell and what makes for a great customer experience in the context of the NDIS.

In one exercise I asked people to share which of the organisation's five values meant the most to them personally and – if they were comfortable – to share why this was so important for them.

Michael, a Sudanese support worker, said that 'Security and Belonging' meant the most to him. As a very young boy he'd been conscripted into the Sudanese Army. He now works in a complex disability unit supporting people just out of prison – and he loves it.

This simple exercise opened up a flood of memorable story-telling. Over the last two years I've really seen how the simple act of storytelling can act as a 'change insulator' within an organisation. Storytelling is the oxygen mask that we all need to apply, to remind ourselves of who we are, what we stand for and why we're still here.

Not another book about culture

So why would I write another book about culture when there is an avalanche of business books and consultants who specialise in corporate change management? Well, there are a few things that distinguish this book from the usual culture rhetoric:

1. This sector needs more practical, affordable tools to address cultural change within a small business model. Corporate change management models struggle to stick in this environment as they can reek of inauthenticity to anyone who has only ever worked for a non-profit. For any disability organisation to succeed, regardless of size, it needs to operate as if it was a successful small business, not a corporate entity. Because disability is a local business. The more closely the organisation understands and serves the needs of the local community, the more likely it is to succeed. Even multi-state providers must adopt a decentralised hub model to be sustainable under the NDIS, not only because disability is a local business, but also because the NDIS is a different animal in every region.

2. The frontline support worker is now the organisation's most important asset and greatest competitive differentiator. Understanding and improving the actual customer experience is now the key success factor. However, the quality of the customer's experience is entirely dependent upon the employee's experience. Yet, as a result of the funding model,

providers are faced with zero funding for training and professional development. This would not be the case for a commercial entity facing an equivalent talent shortage in a highly competitive market.

3. Change management literature is often dominated by theoretical concepts and 'consultant speak'. There is a need to share practical, accessible content using simple language, because culture is the stuff of *being human*. What's the point of writing words that people can't understand? So this book adopts a strategic 'whole-of-organisation' approach to culture in language that can be understood by any reader regardless of their commercial experience or lack thereof.

4. If we can accept that culture is really the internal brand or 'how we do things around here', and that the existing staff team is the most critical target market right now, then we can begin to tailor the messages and prepare a 'whole-of-organisation' action plan to drive engagement with this key target market. Most of the literature available fails to address the unmet needs and pain points of this key target market.

5. This book includes Australian interviews and case studies to extract learnings from leaders in the sector who have thought deeply about the role of culture in their organisations. Every interviewee agreed that culture is now a key business driver. Interestingly, every one of them raised the issue of mission clarity and the need for values to be tied to specific actions and behaviours.

What's ahead?

In this book I provide leaders with the steps and tools to build a high-performance, values-driven culture. It outlines a brand-driven framework for aligning your team, keeping your great people, supporting them and attracting more of them.

The first chapter begins with an overview of the current Australian disability market. The second chapter covers the specific challenges to workplace culture presented by the NDIS. The third chapter outlines a marketing approach, and then we get stuck right into the 5-Step Framework for Building a High-Performance Culture:

- **Step 1) Lead with Vision, Purpose and Integrity:** If your organisation's mission is simply to continue existing then you've forgotten why you're here. People spend ages wordsmithing Mission and Vision Statements and lose touch with the intention behind the words. But, in the right hands, these statements are the absolute foundation stone for a super-engaged workplace. I consider the role of the CEO (and it's not to sit behind a desk), the role of the 'origin story', and the closure of the 'one-stop-shop' disability organisation.

- **Step 2) Build Your Internal Brand:** In my previous book I examined the link between your Vision, the Mission and your organisation's brand values and culture. I still think the brand is the most powerful and underutilised marketing tool in the Australian non-profit sector, but more to the point, this chapter makes the useful distinction between the *internal* brand and the *external* brand. Once you've got this concept, using strategic marketing to drive culture is a no-brainer.

- **Step 3) Recruit for Values:** This is a non-negotiable. Recruit for values, train for skills. Values-based recruitment (and performance management!) will transform your workplace. It requires new skills, new recruitment processes and new role descriptions. It requires a lateral, more entrepreneurial approach to the talent search and a radically different approach to the recruitment process. We discuss how values-based recruitment works both ways, and the mistakes that arise if this doesn't happen.

- **Step 4) Understand Your Current Culture:** In this step we cover how to get 'under the skin' of your organisation. We discuss how collective patterns of thinking drive collective patterns of behaviour or 'how things are done around here'. We look at how to identify and understand the actual patterns of thinking impacting your culture and the key cultural stressors impacting the employee experience. We then ask, what's possible if your team were truly living your brand?

- **Step 5) Create Your Culture Action Plan:** In this chapter I discuss some uncomfortable truths you need to face before you can begin to build an effective plan. We then look at the four principles for building an effective Culture Action Plan that secures cross-functional team 'buy in'.

Finally we chat about toxic indicators and the little things that can make or break an organisation's culture.

How to get the most out of this book

This book is for leaders in the disability sector who know that culture is the game changer.

Like my previous book, you may not need to read it from cover to cover. Some of this stuff you will already know and will probably already be doing – but it's the *how* that I'd ask you to review.

I hope you find new insights in each of the interviews, and I sincerely hope this book delivers beyond your expectations.

With best wishes,

Fran Connelley
Sydney
August 2019

Chapter 1 ▶

The plane without wings

'The NDIS is like a plane that took off before it had been fully built and is being completed while it is in the air.'

Mr J. Whalan, Mr Acton, Dr Jeff Harmer, Independent Capability Review of the NDIS, March 2014

The purpose of this chapter is to give you an overview of the current Australian disability market as context for what follows. Chances are, you may already feel way too familiar with the challenges described here. (This chapter is going to date so fast it scares me – even a month can be a long time in this space!)

The National Disability Insurance Scheme's 'infancy' period is now in its sixth year, and there is little indication that it is maturing. In fact, at times it seems as if this 'plane' has come without wings. Regardless of the number of Productivity Commission reports, 'essential briefings', NDIS forums and legions of well-meaning individuals, the 'wings' have yet to be built.

To describe the Australian disability sector as a complex operating environment is an extreme understatement. Right now this sector would challenge the leadership skills and commercial acumen of any CEO, regardless of their experience. Sadly, it has become such a noisy, volatile, politicised environment that to write anything about the NDIS feels like political commentary, and is quite likely to go out of date the moment the words hit the page.

Over the last two years, whenever I've been asked to speak to boards and community groups about the NDIS I actually have to 'google' what just happened, simply to ensure I am presenting the most relevant, local content.

Leadership spills and a Royal Commission

In the last six years, the NDIS has struggled through the changing politics and policies of four Prime Ministers, four Disability Ministers, two Chief Executives (soon to be a third, as Rob De Luca resigned from the role in May 2019), and another five senior NDIA staff who have resigned in the last three months.

Add to this upheaval is the new Royal Commission. Prior to the Australian election held in May 2019, the Prime Minister Scott Morrison announced a three-year Royal Commission – valued at $538 million – into the disability sector. This overdue move was greatly welcomed by families and disability lobby groups. As I write these words, the newly re-elected Scott Morrison has indicated that addressing the failures in the NDIS will be one of the first priorities of his government and has appointed Stuart Robert as Minister for the NDIS.

The shining light

Back in 2015 the NDIS was still a scheme to capture the imagination. It was a shining light; a world-class reform that we all hoped would deliver genuine choice, control, and the possibility of real inclusion for people with disability.

As a social reform, the NDIS was visionary in its thinking. In excited, perhaps overblown terms I wrote in my previous book, ' ... *for the first time in our history the disability "market" will actually become a market as clients become customers who can directly purchase services of their own choosing, no longer the passive recipients of welfare.'*

In 2015 the early results from the eight 'trial' sites were encouraging. However, as the first state, NSW, commenced the roll out to the full Scheme in July 2016, the payment portal collapsed and it quickly became apparent that the calibre of thinking that conceived the Scheme was not applied to its implementation. The Scheme has been plagued by IT issues ever since, as both participants and providers struggle with the systems.

In fact, the reality of the NDIS bore little resemblance to the trial sites as the speed of the rollout compromised project implementation.

Mixed results for people with disabilities

In fairness, the NDIS has many success stories. According to the latest Quarterly Report, participant satisfaction is currently at 90%. For many people the NDIS is the first time they have received support. As at June 2019, 298,816 participants were benefiting from the Scheme, with 99,537 of those participants receiving support for the first time in their lives.[5]

But for every good news story, there is another story of bureaucratic nightmares, inconsistent decision making and uncertainty. In many of the 'success' stories, the NDIS participant had the advantage of a powerfully articulate parent, carer or local MP advocating in their corner. For people without that advocate or for those who may not have English as a first language, the process can be impenetrable.

In a recent news story, an NDIS participant received a substantial funding package 'for kinds of care that she can't actually use' because her transport allowance no longer applied. Following

---

5   NDIS Quarterly Report, 30 June 2019.

intervention by her local MP, she was given permission to use the funds for taxis which enabled her to actually use her package.[6]

To date, the NDIS Plan utilisation across Australia averages 68%. This reflects the health of the NDIS itself, as it refers to the average percentage of Plan funding that people are spending on their supports. There are a few possible reasons for this low average:

- Thin markets: The inability of participants to actually find providers to deliver the services they are funded for, particularly in regional and remote areas.

- Complexity: Understanding how to access the Scheme and how to access supports can be overwhelming for participants. This particularly applies to those with episodic mental illness and those for whom English is not a first language.

- Or, as the NDIA suggests, it's just a matter of familiarity. Their data confirms that the longer a person is in the Scheme, the more of their Plan they use.

'Participants tend to utilise less of their first plan, compared with their second and subsequent plans, as it takes time to familiarise with the NDIS and decide which supports to use.'

COAG Disability Reform Council Performance Report – National, 30 June 2019

Whatever the reason, the experience has often been that if the package is unspent, the person with the disability may well discover they receive less funding the next year.

Tragically, some of the most vulnerable individuals in this country are now forced to endure the frustration and indignity of having to 'prove' their disability over and over again to complete strangers who may have no prior experience of disability.

One woman with Multiple Sclerosis was rejected by the NDIS a day before she turned 65 (when she would become ineligible for

---

6   *The 7.30 Report*, 10 June 2019.

entry to the NDIS) and eight months after lodging her paperwork to gain access to an NDIS funding package. Jennifer Saunders received a letter from the NDIA on 8 September 2018 requesting various GP and specialist medical reports. She then heard nothing until 2 May 2019. Her request was rejected on the basis that she was 'too mobile'. She did not use a 'wheelie walker' in her home; she used a stool with wheels on it as this was more comfortable for her back. Others with exactly the same condition had been granted access to the Scheme.[7]

On a personal note, over the last three years my own work has taken me to most states of Australia. From firsthand experience, NDIA decision making varies in every state and in just about every region of every state. The inequity and human cost of this inconsistency only creates more stress, frustration and disillusionment for people with disabilities and their families.

These issues go well beyond teething problems or glitches. The effectiveness of any social reform can only be judged by its weakest link. Unfortunately, the weak links are not merely links, they are weak foundations.

Unhelpful rhetoric

In May 2018, I was listening to a senior NDIA staff member speak at a forum in Sydney. It was during her speech that I realised we should probably stop referring to the disability sector as a 'market'. Because it isn't one.

There is an excessive reliance on 'market forces' in the rhetoric that surrounds this reform. Not only is this a disrupted market, given the degree of regulation and price setting it can hardly be called a market at all. So to expect 'market forces' to efficiently allocate resources is unrealistic, head-in-the-sand stuff.

The challenges facing providers are deeply interconnected and entirely disruptive for any legacy-based organisation. They evidence

---

7   *The Australian*, 10 May 2019.

a scheme that has been implemented in far too great a hurry. For simplicity's sake, these challenges are outlined in the diagram below.

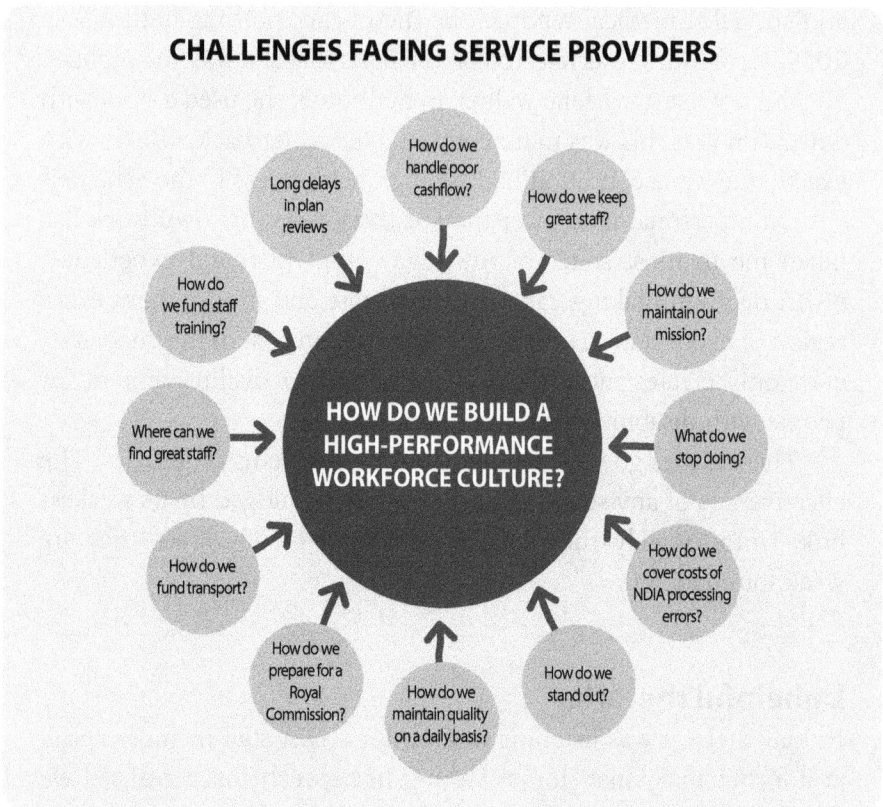

CHALLENGES FACING SERVICE PROVIDERS

How do we handle poor cashflow?

Long delays in plan reviews

How do we keep great staff?

How do we fund staff training?

How do we maintain our mission?

Where can we find great staff?

HOW DO WE BUILD A HIGH-PERFORMANCE WORKFORCE CULTURE?

What do we stop doing?

How do we fund transport?

How do we cover costs of NDIA processing errors?

How do we prepare for a Royal Commission?

How do we maintain quality on a daily basis?

How do we stand out?

Community impacts

In 2012 the COAG report articulated the vision of the National Disability Strategy, referring to 'a new attitude': 'By 2020 we envisage an Australian society that acknowledges the benefits that people with disability bring to all elements of everyday life.'

To date there is little evidence to suggest that the NDIS has changed community attitudes or served to create a more inclusive Australia. Clearly, this attitudinal shift is the responsibility of all institutions, not the NDIA: disability service providers, corporations, government, private, commercial and media. The outdated attitudes will only change when the interfaces between disability and every aspect of our society change.

The opportunity to contribute to society by way of meaningful work cannot be underestimated. '48% of working-age (aged 15–64) people with disability are employed, compared with 79% without disability.'[8] Despite economic participation being a key tenet of the original vision for the NDIS, employment continues to lag: 'As of June 2018, only 2% of NDIS supports for people over 25 years and 5.2 per cent of supports for people 15 to 24 years were for employment.'[9]

Solvency now a major issue for providers

For service providers of all sizes some of the most pressing issues relate to solvency and workforce.

A report released in February 2019 by The Centre for Social Impact (CSI) indicated that a staggering 69% of providers surveyed had received requests for services they were unable to deliver. The report goes on to note the solvency issues facing providers:

> **Concerningly, as the NDIS continues to be rolled out – and providers must adapt to the requirements of the scheme – the financial position of many providers is becoming more precarious. Compared to previous years, more providers are operating at a loss (28%, up from 21% in 2016).**

Long delays in receiving overdue payments from the NDIA for services delivered have seriously threatened the cashflow of many providers.

---

8 www.aihw.gov.au/reports/disability/people-with-disability-in-australia/summary.
9 National Disability Services, State of the Disability Sector Report 2018.

These findings are consistent with several reports released over the last three years.[10] It's fair to say that this writing has been on the wall for some time without any co-ordinated, consistent action to address the many warning signs.

The *State of the Sector Report*, National Disability Services (Dec. 2018) revealed that 54% of providers believe they will have to reduce the quality of their services under the NDIS.

In the same report only 43% of providers were able to meet the escalating demand. In the year prior, it was 53%. This trend is heading in the wrong direction.

Several home care providers have already elected to stop providing NDIS services, most notably Australian Unity, which recently announced that it will scale down its NDIS services in all locations except metropolitan Sydney to focus solely on aged-care services. This move comes only four years after the organisation acquired the NSW Government's home care business for $114 million in 2015.

The end result is that 3000 NDIS participants in regional NSW and Victoria must now find new care providers.

Flawed implementation and pricing

In July 2019 I attended an NDS Essential Briefing Forum, during which the question, 'What issue is most likely to keep you awake at night?' was put to an audience of service providers. An overwhelming 82% of attendees nominated 'NDIS processes and administration' as the issue most likely to keep them awake at night.

At the same forum, another provider shared that his organisation had been waiting three to six months for an urgent plan review. Overall his organisation was owed $8 million in unpaid crisis accommodation.

---

10   Productivity Commission (2017), NDIS Costs Report; Joint Standing Committee on the NDIS, Market Readiness (2018); Australian National Audit Office Report, 2016.

One CEO interviewed for this book said: 'Nobody ever expected the NDIA to be such an impenetrable bureaucracy.' Another CEO explained the gap between the original NDIS vision and the actual NDIS reality as an extreme case of 'capability dissonance'.

With little evidence of sustainable 'market stewardship', the NDIS has served as a blunt instrument, rapidly escalating demand while threatening the supply and quality of services through an inflexible pricing mechanism called the NDIS Price Guide.

A 2018 study of 626 care service providers by the Centre for Social Impact found that 46% of providers listed 'addressing pricing' as their top action for addressing market problems. The abstract for this study goes on to state that 'centralised price setting is detached from service delivery realities, affecting service quality and capability building potential.'[11]

This year, the NDIA began to address the issue. The combined impact of the March 2019 price increases and the indexed increase has meant an overall price rise of 20% to 27% since March and 70% since Scheme commencement.

However, the NDIS Price Guide still does not allow for the costs of the changing business model, or the administrative burden of simply doing business with the NDIA (for example, the payment delays, or the volume of time-consuming plan errors and inconsistencies).

Unclear boundaries, service gaps and cost shifting

It's important to note that pricing and red tape are not the only challenges here.

It appears as if the interface between the NDIS and every state government was overlooked in the rush to achieve the participant targets required by the bilateral funding agreements. So much so

---

11   Carey G, Malbon ER, Weier M, Dickinson H, Duff, G. 'Making Markets Work for Disability Services: The question of price setting'. *Health and Social Care in the Community.* 2019;00:1-8.

that you would forgive anyone for thinking that this major social reform had been conceived in a vacuum.

People living in rural and remote regions and those with complex disabilities are now most at risk, and in many cases are already facing market failure, exacerbated by the hasty withdrawal of mainstream state government services.

In its final report into the National Disability Agreement (Feb. 2019), the Productivity Commission accused the state governments of the 'troubling' behaviour of cost shifting and being deliberately unclear about responsibilities.

The real human cost of these 'unclear boundaries' is hard to measure. The same report evidenced mainstream community services (health, education, mental health, criminal justice, transport and advocacy) actually blocking access to services under the belief that the NDIS should take on the cost.

The boundary issues between health and disability finally received some long overdue clarification in June 2019 when the COAG Disability Reform Council endorsed five major reforms, including the creation of a National Hospital Discharge Action Plan to reduce the number and length of hospital stays by NDIS participants, and agreement that the NDIS should pay for disability-related health supports if they were part of the participant's daily life and resulted directly from their disability (for example, dysphagia supports and swallowing therapy and other essential items).

Workforce shortfall

It appears as if the NDIS was planned without regard to the actual workforce required to meet its own targets. It is widely believed that we need to find another 90,000 workers nationally.

The disability sector is rapidly becoming one of Australia's fastest growing industries. The Federal Government is relying on the 'free market' to meet the demand in its workforce strategy, estimating that one in five jobs will come from this sector. However, the challenging roll-out schedule of the Scheme and the competing demand from other sectors has made it extremely difficult for providers and the NDIA to recruit a sufficiently qualified workforce.

Thin markets getting thinner

Thin markets are those segments where there is a distinct gap between the needs of the participants and the services available. Thin markets are increasingly prevalent in the disability sector as a result of many factors, most significantly the absence of a qualified workforce pool, the challenges of geography and the inflexibility of the NDIA Price Guide.

As I write these words, out in NSW's central west and far west regions it might take you six months to see an allied health professional. This significantly impacts a person's ability to spend their NDIS funding package. Disability services providers are also becoming fewer by the day due to new takeovers and consortiums as providers struggle to find a viable business model that allows for the cost of distance.

As one Dubbo provider remarked to me recently, 'What's the point of getting a $90,000-plus NDIS package if you live in Brewarrina and have nowhere to spend it?'

In September 2018, following an exhaustive national enquiry, the Joint Parliamentary Committee into the NDIS released its report into the market readiness of the Scheme. In addition to several recommendations, the report stated:

> The committee continued to hear that NDIS pricing is hindering market development and growth. More concerning is that, in some instances, pricing has led to service providers discontinuing services to NDIS participants … The committee is

> concerned with the lack of progress on addressing
> the issue of thin markets experienced by some
> groups. The thin markets identified are not
> new; it is now urgent that the NDIA intervene
> beyond making small adjustments to pricing.

Thin markets are not only geographic. They are prevalent within Aboriginal communities, within non-English speaking communities, for those who may require higher, more complex support needs, and across the allied health market.

So where are we now?

The NDIS is now available across Australia and the transition is nearly complete. The 12th NDIS Quarterly Report (June 2019) indicates $18 billion has been spent since Scheme inception. Over 298,800 participants have now been supported and just over 99,500 are receiving support for the first time. There were 21,510 registered providers, of whom only 57% were active. Sole traders comprise 46% of providers. Interestingly, 80% to 95% of NDIA payments are received by 25% of those registered providers, reflecting the concentration levels of this market.[12]

From 1 July 2018, the NDIS Quality and Safeguarding framework ('the NDIS Commission') began operating in New South Wales and South Australia, adding new layers of compliance for providers with increased reporting of audits and behaviour support measures. It's still early days, however once again there appears to have been little thought given to the systemic interface between the NDIS and the new Commission. It commenced in Victoria, Queensland, Tasmania, ACT and NT in July 2019 and will begin in WA in July 2020.

---

12   COAG Disability Reform Council Performance Report – National, 30 June 2019.

The compliance requirements are actually having the effect of deregulating the market. In the nine months to September 2018 over 200 registered providers quit the Scheme because it was no longer viable for their businesses.[13] Allied health providers who are already accredited with their own professional body are now exiting the Scheme because they cannot afford to be registered providers under the NDIS.

With the new Royal Commissions into Aged Care (Commonwealth) and Mental Health (Victoria) and the newly announced Royal Commission into the Disability Sector (Commonwealth), it is likely that in 2020 the complexity of the operating environment will only increase.

---

13   *The Australian*, 12 January 2019.

Summary

▶ The disability sector is an extremely volatile and complex operating environment.

▶ Demand for services outstrips the capacity to supply.

▶ Persistent implementation and administration issues have placed a significant cost burden on providers. The heavy cost of these issues means that providers are funding the NDIS implementation.

▶ There is a major workforce shortfall.

▶ Unclear boundaries have created confusion and cost shifting across government services (health, education, criminal justice, mental health, advocacy, and so on).

▶ Those most at risk of market failure are people living in rural and remote regions, and people with complex intellectual disabilities.

▶ The NDIS has made thin markets even thinner.

▶ Market forces are unable to efficiently allocate resources due to price controls and the prevalence of thin markets.

▶ As at June 2019, the NDIS has funded $18 billion in supports.

▶ The interface between the NDIS Commission and the NDIS is lacking.

Interview

Robyn Kaczmarek, Co-Founder Co-Owner and Co-operative Development Officer at The Co-operative Life

The Co-operative Life is Australia's first (and only) worker-owned co-operative in social care services. Robyn founded TCL after becoming disillusioned with the low pay and poor conditions she experienced as a direct support worker for an aged-care agency. The Co-operative Life began in 2013 with a single employee and an overdraft of $15,000 that has never been used. Today, there are over 25 members and 85 staff who have the opportunity to become a co-owner under the TCL Australia banner and they are growing every day.

How did TCL begin?

In 2008 I needed to find flexible, part-time work so I decided to go into aged care working for an agency. I was basically left on my own to go out and see people after I'd completed my basic training. This meant turning up to somebody's front door without any prior introduction and figuring out a care plan. Then the contract would end and you'd have to explain that this was the last day and there'd be no other communication. I don't think that is very fair for the support worker or the person receiving the care.

So I decided to become a case manager and get private customers. But as soon as you do this, you need staff, and I did not want to start an agency because I believed we really needed to take better care of our staff and make sure people have good jobs.

I began researching overseas models and found Home Care Associates in New York and Sunderland Home Care Associates in the UK. These models gave the staff a voice in their working environment and they could also all share if there was a surplus. I wanted to start something like that here. That's where the co-operative idea came from.

What are the advantages of a co-operative model and is it financially sustainable under the NDIS?

It's a really good model because it's local and it involves people that are usually passionate about what they want. But it's not well known in Australia so you have to do a fair bit of education for people when they first join the business.

A co-operative is just another legal business structure. It acts as any other business would under the NDIS. We have the same inputs, costs and outputs. The advantages of the model are related to the ownership principle which is then related to the democratic principle where every member has a vote. We are an employee-owned co-operative. After a six-month probationary period you can elect to become a member and shareholder. No matter how many shares you hold you can only ever have one vote. So it has a level of equality in it. The advantages for a business are that people do actually have a say in the running of the business. That's a really strong incentive for people to come and work for us rather than another organisation where they may just get a number and a roster.

Can you give me a brief outline of your organisational structure and the thinking behind it?[14]

We're going to a hub-and-spoke model so we can begin to scale. We will have a top entity called 'TCL Australia' and it will be the back office: handling invoices, payroll, accreditations, HR and the membership. Then we have satellite entities: TCL Sydney, TCL New England, and we're hoping to expand into Adelaide, Melbourne and Canberra. Each satellite will have its own committee, and self-manage with assistance from TCL Australia.

We are working with UTS to build a 'business in a box' model that can be easily introduced when there is a need for a local

---

14   TCL's Org Chart and Purpose statement – including values, co-operative principles, shared goals and membership details – can be found in *The Workplace Culture & the NDIS Handbook*, available for download from www.fcmarketing.com.au.

co-owned social care service in a community. This could be a group of workers in an area who want to have autonomy and share ownership of the business, or it could be because a service is closing due to market failure and the workers want to continue the services.

We are also looking at primary health in relation to aged care. When the NDIS and aged care don't work, where do you go? Emergency departments? As a direct care provider we see firsthand what happens when those connections are not made. The GP and the pharmacy are the two things that stay constant for a person who needs support when living in the community. The social care provider is an important link in making sure the person needing support stays in touch with their GP and pharmacy.

What are the major changes that you're seeing in the disability market and what impact do you think this is having on employees?

Customers are no longer sticky. They can walk with just two weeks' notice. That's *huge* on employee job security.

The second thing is that we can't supply everybody. If we want to provide a bespoke service then we have to have enough funding to cover that service. We have self-managed teams and we have to ensure we have enough hours in those teams to enable them to do their job well. So we can't be doing ad hoc hours. If a person wants this type of service it is referred onto larger providers who have the capacity and scope

In future I think there will be a lot of market failure as organisations of all sizes realise they can't afford to run how they've been running. That was our experience in the New England area where 26 employees were going to be sacked as an organisation decided to pull out of the disability space. It also meant that up to 40 to 50 people would be left without support. So we were invited to step in. We made sure that people were seamlessly able to transition their employment and we were able to take on all their NDIS service agreements and keep the services going.

What role does your culture play at TCL?

It's actually *huge*. Not only do we have the direct care support side of what we do, we have a parallel program running called, '*Act Like an Owner*'.

'*Act Like an Owner*' has four underlying principles that all staff have to understand:

- The business model.

- The economic model: how much goes in and how much goes out.

- The four core processes of our policies and procedures.

- The operating parameters: they need to have an understanding of the environment we're operating in and where we're heading.

So there is complete transparency around our business processes and direction.

The problem is how do you roll this out with no money for training? So we use Slack and Zoom. I'm now making a podcast for education on worker co-operatives. This tells our staff our purpose, our vision, the seven co-operative principles and what makes us different, being a co-owned business. It's also telling staff about our member value proposition (MVP) and why they should become a member of the co-operative. It's just really constant messaging all the time and we always cover our culture at induction.

The whole business runs on the same IT system which is really crucial. As we move towards a self-managed model IT integration is very important. We have been doing this manually and know what works, so we will use IT to automate what we do, so we can then give senior staff more time to coach other staff members in self-management

Face to face is incredibly difficult. We're in the Glen Innes area – and staff have to travel 45 minutes just to meet. So we have to be thinking how to use the internet and the cloud to get the messages through.

Getting people to think like an owner really changes the whole power structure, the communication flow, and really everything doesn't it?

It took me five years to understand that – but yes that's the key pin. It's not that we're a co-operative; it's because we're helping them to think like an owner. I had the idea that ownership was the key factor – that came from the co-operatives. It comes down to the business being owned by the employees.

How do you bring your values alive for your staff, members and co-owners?

Repeat them and live them! We also performance manage by our values. It really is just a matter of constant reminders and constant use. It's taken us four years to figure it out and we've really only put our values in place this year and we know now exactly what they are. We know what works and we need to be actively applying that. Having said that, we're limited by the NDIS training budget. So we're now offering members paid training that is specific to their job requirements. We want our members to have the training they need to manage the myriad issues that come up in their daily working lives when dealing with our customers.

How do you hang on to quality staff?

Give them enough hours. People need enough hours to have a decent living wage. We are an organisation that pays on time. We pay above award and offer bonuses for those staff who contribute time and effort into making sure the co-operative is the best place to work and the best place to receive support services.

I think it's crucial that we think about work for the future. We need to ensure that people have a job where they can bring up a family, put aside some savings and then retire well. Disability and aged care are wonderful sectors to work in but we need to ensure that people can raise a family and do those things. If we take that away from people it will lead to a crumbling of society.

How do you generate culture in remote teams?

In addition to using Slack and Zoom and our new podcasts, we have face-to-face meetings to connect with our people. Our Regional Directors have regular meals with their teams where they take all the team out and just talk. We have a Lead Support Worker in each team who works in the field, so we allocate a budget for them each year to have lunches with all the teams. It's informal.

How important is your role as Co-op Development Officer in driving culture?

As we are working towards self-management, we are also restructuring the organisation towards a flatter hierarchy. As a worker-owned co-op, we all have different jobs, but no person's job is any more important than another person's job. We are all interconnected and need each other to make sure we deliver what we promise. In essence we are our own small ecosystem that is part of a bigger system, and we all need to work together.

I stepped down as CEO as our board decided that we will have a management team run the day-to-day operations rather than having one person as CEO do this. We have just implemented this process where the board decides what and how to do things and the management team carry these out. My role as CDO is to keep an eye on the big picture and the co-operative ethos and principles, and to educate and inspire other members to put these principles into their daily work.

Self-management and co-operatives go hand in hand – some people don't want to self-manage, they want to be given directions, so we need to work slowly, steadily, bit by bit encouraging people to take on the responsibility. It's very much about directing it and then letting them experience it so people have their own 'a-ha' moments.

What's been your experience with self-managed teams? Do you believe it's the way forward for disability and aged care?

I do. It doesn't have to be in a co-operative model but you've got to figure out what makes the team tick. I know the Buurtzorg model but I don't think it will work here because the Australian funding model is different.

Our role is very much a social care model and there's a lot of training associated with that. When you have no budget for that it's really hard, so it's going to go even slower. I've been reading about self-managed teams since before the Buurtzorg era: in manufacturing it's hard – and they're all in the one room working the same hours. So multiply the difficulty of putting that into aged care and disability with remote workers and distance. That is why our IT system is really crucial as it allows connection and communication. It's taken us five years to work out how to do it.

What's the next step for TCL?

As we grow we may look to become a co-operative enterprise; a federation of co-operatives with different membership classes. What we need is a system where a community of local workers provide the ongoing care and support for those who need it. We need to be looking at ways to do this that are simple and work for both the staff and the customer. I think co-operatives are a good option.

We wouldn't be here if it wasn't for the NDIS, and individual budgets are a fantastic step. We just need to make it work for us. As a newly established organisation we did not start from a negative position of having to figure out cashflow because we didn't rely on bulk funding. We did not borrow any money, or have to rely on any grant funding. We started with one customer and one staff member and built the business around that.

We had to have low overheads as we had no money in reserve. So we never had that mentality of dipping into reserves to fund current work. That is probably our biggest advantage: that we'd figured out how to run the business as a business.

Our hub-and-spoke model will be sustainable because we are actually scaling and diversifying. Offering aged care and disability has to be part of the mix of any business that wants to be successful.

Interview

Kerry Stubbs, CEO and Managing Director, Northcott

Northcott is one of Australia's largest not-for-profit disability service organisations, supporting people throughout NSW and the ACT. It began in 1929 as The NSW Society for Crippled Children, formed by Sydney City Rotary in response to the polio epidemic during the Great Depression. Today, Northcott employs over 2000 staff and provide services to over 13,500 people with disability, their families and carers each year.

Kerry Stubbs has been CEO and Managing Director of Northcott for the last 12 years. She is a Director of The SpineCare Foundation Ltd, Northcott Innovation Ltd, AsOne Therapy Ltd, Northcott Supported Living and CRC for Water Sensitive Cities, and Chair of their Audit and Risk Committee. Kerry is a Member of the Board of Trustees for Western Sydney University and Chair of their Finance and Investment Committee. She was recently appointed Deputy Chancellor of Western Sydney University.

Kerry, what do you think are the biggest challenges facing the disability sector now? If you had one key message for providers right now, what would it be?

There are a number of challenges facing the sector right now but I think my key message for providers would be that now is the time to refocus on your purpose as an organisation. What's the reason you exist? What is your mission? Are you making sure that whatever you do in these turbulent times that you are still focusing on your mission? If you can't deliver services sustainably, then perhaps it's time to consider doing something else.

This week I attended a CEO Discussion Forum where the NSW Ageing and Disability Commissioner Robert Fitzgerald spoke. He also encouraged organisations to refocus on their mission.

His message was simple: Organisations need to be clear on *why* they're here; what is it that you're trying to do?

In terms of challenges facing the sector, one of the key challenges is around staff. We know that we have staff shortages and that these shortages will exist across the sector. We're experiencing competition from other providers as well as the aged care sector.

I'm seeing a lot of churn in the sector as people move from one organisation to another. But that's a zero sum game. Certainly I can understand that people are keen to improve their position, and we've been able to secure some great new talent where someone might have been unhappy with another provider and have been attracted by our reputation.

However, it's not good for the customer if people are moving all the time. As an industry we need to think about how to grow the overall disability workforce on a longer term basis.

Along with other large providers we've been meeting with the NSW Department of Industry to discuss these issues. I sit on the Board of the University of Western Sydney and I'm constantly talking about the need for a larger care workforce. However, this needs an industry-wide, co-ordinated approach to workforce planning. We need a national workforce strategy but I think we also need to address this on a state-by-state basis.

How do you address the issue of attracting future talent?

We're constantly rethinking how to do this. There's also a big retention piece: how to hang onto our quality people.

This is particularly challenging for therapists. We've been looking carefully at what it is that they value and how to attract and retain more therapists. We now offer 10 days of study leave for therapists and we're looking at different recruitment methods.

For disability support workers we're looking at group recruitment methods and various forms of internal and external referral networks.

We're doing pretty well in attracting management talent. We've got great people and have some excellent processes in place.

We also take on students and work experience students. We have a strong Aboriginal staff workgroup and a Reconciliation Action Plan to both attract more Aboriginal staff and to better support our Indigenous customers. We also have a workplace inclusion group who focus on attracting more people with disability into our workforce.

We currently offer great leadership training and development programs for all levels of managers from frontline supervisors to senior executives.

What role does your culture play at Northcott? How do you keep your values 'front of mind'? How do you keep your diverse teams 'connected'?

We've got a number of different projects in place to make sure our culture stays front of mind through Northcott Innovation. The question is, *What is the Northcott way? Does everybody know what that means?*

We are currently using our subsidiary, Northcott Innovation, to work on some projects that are all about focus on the customer and the way staff need to work to best support our customers. These projects are a key part of our strategic plan.

We also run the employee opinion survey using the Voice Project out of Macquarie Uni.

A particular issue for us has been the integration of over 1000 employees since 2017 after the NSW state government's withdrawal. That's been a big cultural change piece for us.

On a separate issue, we have a great new intranet. We also do things like expecting all our managers and administration staff to work in frontline positions for at least one day every year.

More broadly, across the organisation we have a number of cultural engagement strategies, all of which are carefully measured and the outcomes monitored for progress.

Have you changed your organisational structure to better support your culture and the customer experience under the NDIS?

Not yet. We did change two years ago when we absorbed the state government employees, however we will have a senior executive planning day in a few weeks' time to review our organisational structure and bed things down.

We've done a lot of work around roles and responsibilities and really focusing on the role of the frontline supervisor to see how we can reduce their burden. With all the operational changes so much extra stuff has been loaded onto them when really we want them to be able to spend more time getting to know our customers and leading good practice for our staff.

We've implemented a practice leadership stream offering structured training and on-the-job mentoring, particularly in our accommodation services. We're looking carefully at how we can lead practice on the job.

Within our quality and safeguarding group we've set up a group of experienced managers as a support group that staff can ring for on-the-job advice. The idea came from one of our Quality and Safeguarding Managers, Jill McGinty, a very experienced practitioner.

In terms of agency staff, it's less than it used to be. It's currently about 10% to 12% of our workforce. We have had a high use of agency staff in the Specialist Supported Living homes we took over from FACS, which are staffed with nursing staff, but we are currently in the process of hiring more nursing staff to replace agency.

However, I recently completed a 'listening tour' of our families around the state and I know that families don't want agency staff or short-term casual staff in their homes. They want to know who is supporting them.

Kerry, what do you think is the impact of the focus on quality and compliance on the actual customer experience?

It's a matter of being aware of the risks. We don't want to be so risk averse that the experience of the customer, their ability to make decisions and choices is actually inhibited. I regularly read the policies and procedures to ensure that their freedoms and that the dignity of risk is protected as much as possible.

The second point is that time completing paperwork is time away from the customer. We need to use technology to ensure administration is as seamless as possible, and assists rather than detracts from the frontline management role. As a result, our frontline supervisor or 'Service Co-ordinator' position is a full-time role. Under the state government, they were 40% admin and 60% rostered on shift. However, they need to be full-time supervisory to ensure they have the time to be leading practice, making sure that staff are coached, trained and serving our customers.

As CEO, what role do you play in driving the culture at Northcott and how does this work on a practical, daily basis?

There are two roles I play. Firstly, I spend a lot of time talking to staff, and listening to what they have to tell me. I try to visit all sites at least one day every year, and I have just finished touring the state to present the three-year strategic plan to staff and listen to any concerns they have. I make sure I'm approachable, accessible. It's a *'personal presence'* role. They know they can email me any time or talk to me in person if they wish.

My second role is about asking questions if I don't think what we're doing is in accordance with our culture. As a CEO, my role isn't to be a 'do-er'. My role is to make people think; to question what we're doing.

We have a weekly executive meeting. If someone can't explain why we're doing something, then we shouldn't be doing it. If they can't explain how what we're doing is consistent with our culture, then we also shouldn't be doing it.

Finally, how does Northcott measure the staff and customer experience?

For staff satisfaction we're building a business intelligence system which looks at common measures such as sick leave, workers compensation claims, injuries and incidents – and we also have the Voice Project survey which I previously mentioned.

In terms of how we measure the customer experience, we look at complaints and incidents, we have an annual customer engagement survey and we look at customer goals attainment. As part of the Ability First Australia we've assembled a market research panel of 400-plus customers and carers that will enable us to test new ideas, new products and allow us to understand the new issues that we need to be on top of in terms of improving the customer experience within different segments of those groups. This is an Australia-first initiative which we are currently piloting with an external market research company.

Kerry, do you have any final comments you'd like to add?

The only other thing I'd like to say is that I'm more and more convinced that the Quality & Safeguarding Commission will drive more positive culture change than anything else. We've just been through our first third-party accreditation and certainly there are issues around reducing the administrative burden, but I'm hopeful that we will see big improvements.

My message to the sector is that the NDIS Commission will bring positive culture change if we work with it and embrace it.

Chapter 2 ▶

Workplace culture and the NDIS

'The greatest danger in times of turbulence is not the turbulence –
it is to act with yesterday's logic.'

Peter F. Drucker

Regardless of your organisation's size, workplace culture is the game changer. In the perfect storm of the NDIS, it is the organisation's culture that's going to hold it together or split it into silos. Over the last four years I've seen silos within the same organisation between directors, between layers of leadership, between regions, between administrative and frontline teams, between marketing departments and everyone else, and between allied staff and support workers.

As part of my Strategic Marketing Program, I typically interview attendees before the first workshop to understand the cultural and personality dynamics operating in the organisation. I recall interviewing a therapist two years ago who worked for a large disability service provider. She kept referring to her therapist colleagues as 'the other professionals'. When asked if the frontline support workers were also professionals, the answer was a flat 'no'.

Language reflects culture, and culture reflects what we collectively value.

It is culture that determines the actual working environment: things like whether rosters are fair, whether the workplace is healthy and safe, absenteeism, staff retention rates, median staff age, ratio of cancellations, the distance from frontline to CEO, whether a quality service is being delivered to the customer, how people (employees as well as customers) are welcomed, and how they exit the organisation.

With the Disability Royal Commission about to shine a spotlight on abusive, violent workplace practices, it's important that leaders begin gathering firsthand information about workplace quality as well as customer service quality and then monitor that information at a point in time and as trending data.

And yet (still) so many organisations have only the annual 'staff satisfaction survey' to measure cultural health.

One Tuesday morning recently I was chatting with the General Manager of Client Services for a multi-state disability services provider, during the morning tea break in my Culture Masterclass. She was an extremely well qualified, talented woman who had joined her organisation only four months earlier, having come from a large 'for-profit' environment. Passionate about her organisation's mission, she brought strong commercial experience and significant customer experience skills. She commented to me:

> **I never wanted to be the sort of manager who was too busy to look up when my staff came to my door, or one who would stare glassy eyed when they presented me with both a problem and their suggested solution, or someone who worked until 3 am just to complete another report for our board. But that's who I've become.**

I suggested to her that a line needs to be drawn in the sand. This was not sustainable for her, for her team, or for her organisation.

But I'm getting ahead of myself …

The way we work must change

Before I dive into the specific challenges to culture faced by disability providers, it may be helpful to get some broader context.

Gallup's *State of the Global Workplace 2017* data showed that, globally, organisations are moving away from hierarchical, function-based structures towards more flexible, team-based arrangements, connected via online platforms. Authority is being decentralised as businesses reorganise for speed and agility in order to stay competitive.

The same report found that only 14% of employees in Australia and New Zealand are engaged in their work. Australian workplaces rate among the lowest in the world when it comes to employee engagement and satisfaction, ranking seventh out of 11 global regions.

More people than ever are digitally connected, and yet so many people don't have the skills to have difficult or meaningful conversations. The sheer quantity of data is triumphing over the quality of connections. This lack of employee engagement has serious implications for workplace health, personal wellbeing and customer trust.

The 2019 Pro Bono Australia Salary Survey of 1421 not-for-profit leaders found that 46% of people reported feeling 'stressed' and demonstrated lower levels of engagement, and 80% saw their work as demanding – a group labelled as 'stretched'. The highest proportion of CEO respondents came from the disability sector.

In the Australian disability sector, the trend towards decentralisation has been fast tracked by the NDIS funding model. It requires the service provider to have the technology and organisational structures in place to enable self-direction, retain a mission focus, and achieve sustainability within an extremely low margin environment and with constantly shifting goalposts.

Many new market entrants have based their business models on online platforms (for example, Hire UP, Home Care Heroes, and Hit 100) which should enable more profitability.

The self-managed teams model from the UK is another way to accommodate the need for greater competitive agility. The decentralised structure requires employees to have a higher level of self-awareness, the skills training to self-manage successfully, and the resources to cope with a more flexible roster. (The Co-operative Life is a fabulous example of how to make this work within the Australian context. Robyn Kaczmarek is interviewed later in this book.)

It's fair to say that the NDIS has forced all disability providers to review their business models and adopt a more commercial focus. However, the ability to pay a fair wage, offer regular shifts, provide training and professional development and still accommodate the choices and expectations of the NDIS participants is particularly difficult if you're also struggling with persistent solvency issues.

The Australian disability workforce

The majority of the disability workforce is female (76% compared to 46% in the wider Australian workforce[15]), over 45, with a certificate-level qualification. This does not reflect the emerging needs of NDIS participants for support workers with similar ages and interests.

The significant workforce shortfall referred to in the previous chapter is readily apparent from the annual market survey of 626 providers in the NDS State of the Sector Report (Dec. 2018):

> **Nearly two thirds of respondents (63%) reported extreme or moderate difficulty in recruiting disability support workers, up from 42% in 2017. Managers and supervisors moved into the 'difficult-to-recruit' category this year for over half of respondents, compared to around**

---

15   NDS State of the Sector Report December 2018.

one third in 2017. The most acute recruitment difficulties reported in 2018, as in the two previous years, were for allied health positions.

The National Disability Services' Australian Disability Workforce Report, released in July 2018, indicated rapid net employment growth in the previous financial year of 13.8%, as a result of a significant rise in casual employment. In March 2018, casuals accounted for nearly half of the total workforce. Casual employment is growing at an increasing rate. This is particularly true for small to medium-sized providers. The impacts of an increasingly casualised workforce on the culture of an organisation can be considerable, and smaller providers are at risk.

Workforce turnover is also increasing. Casuals' turnover rate is now at 8.55% per quarter, and the rate for permanent staff is 5.2% per quarter.

Of growing concern is the declining trend in working hours in NSW, ACT and WA. Disability support workers need hours. They need rosters that offer a decent continuity of work so they can earn a decent wage, raise a family and set aside some savings.

As Michael Chester (UnitingCare West) remarked in his interview:

I believe that we have an obligation to keep the issue of the working poor on the radar for everybody … for politicians, the NDIA and every provider in the sector. If the current trend continues, we have the possibility of a new working poor emerging in the ranks of disability providers around the country.

The Federal Government's recently released workforce strategy does little to actually value the work done by the disability workforce or to attract the numbers required to fulfil the demand within this sector.

'All my staff are ex-ADHC'

Before the NDIS, this was an outdated, 'broken' system. Decades of government funding had created an inefficient market with heavy administration costs and lengthy delays on equipment and services. Disability providers typically relied on government for at least 85% of their total revenue.

In 2008, as a marketing and fundraising consultant newly arrived in the disability sector, I recall asking a CEO whether he was concerned that 85% of his funding came from government. Didn't he feel vulnerable? His reply shocked me deeply. He looked at me and said, 'Why should I be worried? I'm ex-ADHC. All my staff are ex-ADHC.' The Department of Ageing, Disability and Home Care (ADHC) was the state government department in NSW responsible for funding disability services at that time. Financial security was clearly not an issue for this CEO.

The new key relationship

The following diagram outlines the new key relationship for a provider's financial sustainability. It also shows how the new funding model drives the new business model.

The new key relationship

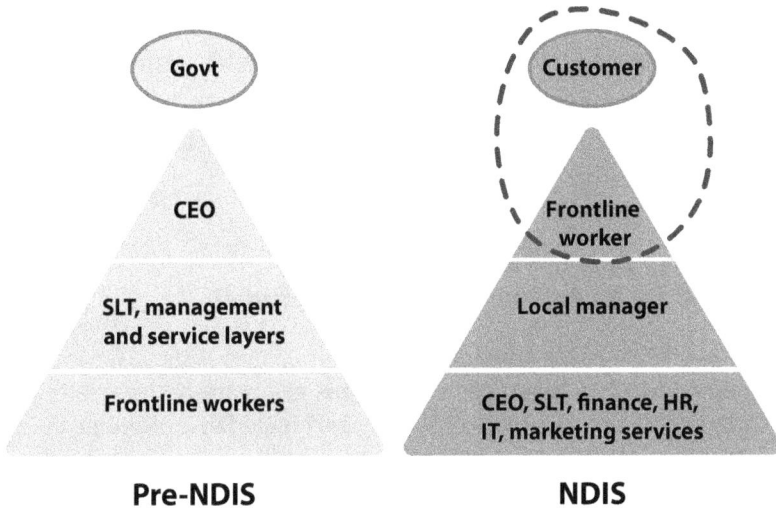

Pre-NDIS

NDIS

Pre NDIS: The key relationship was the one that the CEO held with the respective state government funder. Every layer of the organisation was there to serve that relationship. The organisational structure and the language reflected that relationship. The frontline support worker was at the base of the pyramid and customer or 'service user' did not even appear in the structure. The organisation was measured on *outputs*, not *outcomes*.

Post NDIS: The key relationship for financial sustainability is now the one between the frontline support worker and the customer or 'NDIS participant'. Every other layer in the organisation exists to support the quality of that relationship.

The disability customer is not looking for a transaction. Despite the rhetoric, the NDIS is not Medicare. They are simply looking for someone they can trust.

As a result, what your frontline staff member feels, your customers are going to feel. If they don't feel heard, valued and supported, then neither will your customers. Many organisations have tried to drive a commercial focus throughout their frontline teams without thought to the actual employee experience. It's a waste of time and money to conduct customer experience training until you really understand the employee's experience and your actual workplace culture. If you do, you may be simply adding another layer of protocols and admin for people who are already exhausted and possibly burnt out.

'Hey Fran, do you know you're on in Terrigal?'

In early 2018 I was working with a client in Queensland when I received a text message from another client attending an NDS training forum in Terrigal, NSW. Her text included a photo of my face with these two pyramids on the big screen at the front of a conference room with a few hundred people in it. It took me a few minutes to realise that the consultant presenting the session (whom I had never heard of) was showing a training video from my website. I decided that this was a compliment. And hey, I'd made all my videos free to access.

Over the last two years, I've found that, for many people, this diagram is the first time they **actually see why** their organisational structure has to change or why it feels like their organisation is being turned upside down.

Workforce quality

The most important asset for any disability provider is now the quality and composition of their workforce. Some of the factors required to ensure the strength, quality and fit of the new key relationship are:

- The organisation communicates transparently and respectfully with every customer, carer and family member at every interaction.

- The employee has the ability to consistently deliver a values-based service with every interaction.

- The employee has sufficient training and support to enable them to thrive in their role. They feel safe all of the time.

- The employee has the right job skills and experiences to match the customer's needs.

- The employee is the right age, demographic and personality profile to match the customer's needs.

- The employee is sufficiently flexible in their hours to adjust to fit the customer's needs.

People with disabilities want the choice of more in-home and in-community support rather than the traditional centre-based model. They deserve access to mainstream services. They want to be able to pursue their choice of work, life skills, hobbies and passions, whether it's going to the movies, travelling overseas, becoming a DJ or a rap artist, or trying photography.

Service providers need workers who can make this happen, who are able to work remotely, unsupervised, while connected by mobile technology.

When you weigh all this against the backdrop of a workforce shortage, the fact that many workers will explore opportunities to work for themselves, and the fact that many customers will prefer to hire directly rather than use a 'middle man' (who may provide different people on their doorstep every day), then the scale of the workforce challenge faced by disability providers begins to become apparent.

The cultural challenges facing disability providers

The typical CEO of a disability service organisation must deal with several cultural challenges. For simplicity's sake, some of these are summarised in the diagram below.

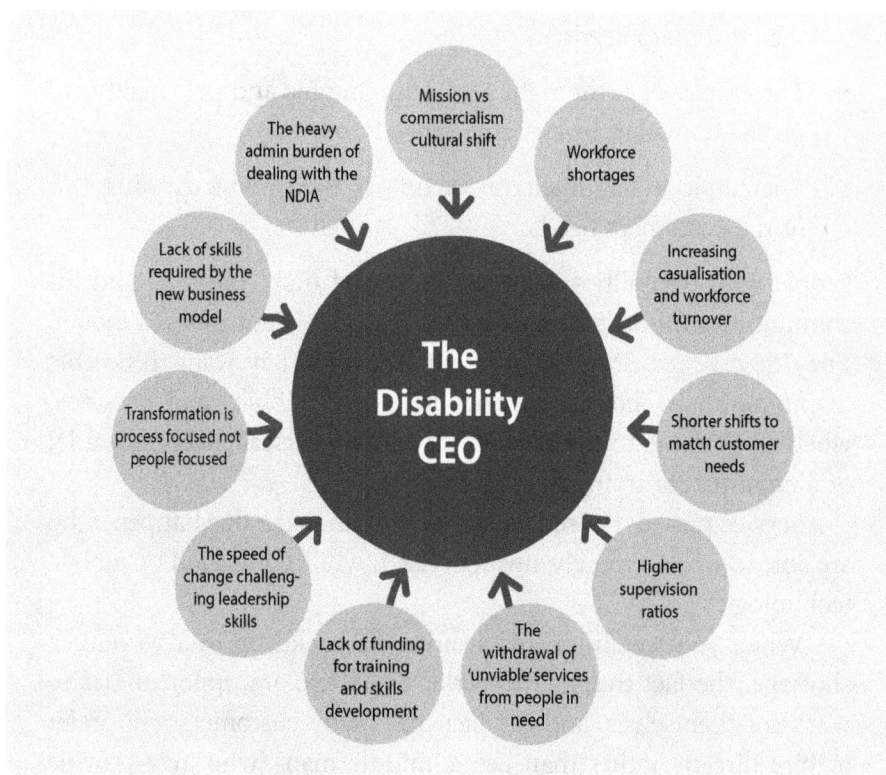

Summary

▶ Culture either holds organisations together or splits them into silos.

▶ Language reflects culture and culture reflects what we collectively value.

▶ Organisations must decentralise structures and decision making.

▶ The disability workforce does not reflect emergent customer needs.

▶ Workforce turnover and casualisation are increasing.

▶ The issue of the working poor must be addressed.

▶ The new key relationship requires a new business model.

▶ We need new measures for workforce 'quality'.

▶ There are significant cultural challenges facing service providers.

Interview

Rob White, CEO, Elise Taylor, GM Strategy & Development, and Frank Sedmack, GM People & Culture, Cerebral Palsy Alliance

Cerebral Palsy Alliance was started by a group of parents in 1945 as The Spastic Centre. It was the first organisation of its type in the world for people with cerebral palsy. CPA provides family-centred therapies, life skills programs, equipment and support for people and their families living with cerebral palsy and other neurological and physical disabilities. Over the last four years, CPA grew from 55 sites to 112 sites operating throughout metropolitan, regional and rural NSW and the ACT.

Rob White has been CEO of CPA since 2000. Elise Taylor (nee Stumbles) manages a diverse portfolio including strategic planning, quality and organisational development. She led the organisation through the NDIS trial site participation and the internal change management program. She has been with the organisation for 17 years. Frank Sedmack also joined CPA 17 years ago. Since then he has renegotiated their enterprise awards, developed their strategic workplace plan and introduced the Employee Value Exchange program.

What do you think are the biggest challenges facing disability providers right now? If you had one key message for them, what would it be?

Rob: I think the biggest challenge for us all is workforce. I argue that the NDIS is a 10-year reform. I think we are in the sixth year of the 10-year reform. Three years of trials and now, in NSW and ACT, we are into year three of the roll out. Everybody is working hard to make it as easy as possible, but the reforms are still pretty clunky. Most organisations have spent the last couple of years trying to get their back-of-house operations right. If you looked at the old state funding model, our organisation is unusual because we are pretty good at fundraising. Our breakdown was about 60% government money, 20% fundraising and 20% other. So we used to receive four payments a year, in advance. Under the NDIS we are doing over 20,000 transactions in a month. We have a great finance and IT team who worked really hard to make that work.

Workforce shortage is a huge issue, an issue for every disability organisation in Australia, because of the amount of new workforce required for this funding scheme (and we are competing with health and aged care).

The other key issue for me is that organisations need to be focused on their mission. We don't see ourselves as an arm of government. We have stuck to our mission and we are very clear about it. We exist for people with cerebral palsy, but we do also see people who have other complex physical and neurological disabilities.

With these huge reforms I worry that, for some organisations, their mission is simply to continue existing. Unless you are very clear on *why* you exist, your point of differentiation, then you may as well merge. Then you get all the advantages of scale and sharing resources. We will see a lot more of that.

How do you see the CEO's role in creating culture and communicating vision? How do you do that at CPA?

Rob: I think culture is such an integral part of any organisation. It is tied up with everything that we do and we say. Going back to basics and being very clear about why we exist and having very clear values. Reinforcing that in how you recruit, how you advertise, how you orientate and how you bring new people on board into your organisation. It's so critical.

The CEO and board have to get that culture right and we do that in a range of ways. We are a very regionalised service with about 112 sites, so you've got to get the message out there as best you can. Continually reinforcing it in that middle layer of management is critical.

Elise: If the emphasis of this book is around culture then I think the number one challenge is being brave enough to hold true to your culture. We are having very active, challenging conversations around this and I think that's really healthy.

If I looked at what destabilised or worried our staff a few years ago it was, 'Because we are an NDIS provider now does that mean we are not a non-profit that is here to do good anymore? Does that mean that we are no longer here to make a difference? Because that's what we signed up for.'

And that is such a huge part of our DNA. We are here to make a difference and do good.

We know that we are more than the NDIS. Our strategy is about making a difference and creating impact. We are all a bit NDIS weary. We had to get in the trenches, and we are now coming out of that.

I strongly believe that what is going to motivate and re-energise our staff is going back to that narrative of who we are, why we exist, what impact we want to create and how we want to make a difference. It is part of your cultural story. So I think organisations that can tell that story and be really clear on that will keep steering a good ship.

Culturally, having that mission clarity is very important. *That* is the tight rope: making sure that you are living to your core values. Our mission and our vision are the things we have to keep going back to. Right now it is *really* important.

How has your organisational structure changed in response to the NDIS? How does it support your culture through the pace of change?

Rob: We have more sites than we used to and more localised services. The executive structure is much the same, although we have added a business development manager.

We upgraded our marketing function. We have a wonderful new marketing GM with a really competent team and we are now marketing for clients. In the past we didn't really want to promote ourselves to clients because we couldn't meet the needs of our waiting lists. The marketing function was more about marketing to government and fundraising to corporate. Now it is more about marketing to clients as well.

We invested a lot into the change program. We just took on 58 government group homes. These were people joining our organisation who were long term with FACS (The Department of Families and Community Services). I said to my staff, 'Imagine if one day, after you've been working for FACS for 20 years, you discover that you're now going to be working for CPA.'

We really concentrated on that change process to make them feel welcome, to bring them into the organisation and work with them to then become part of the Cerebral Palsy Alliance culture and family. You also want to ensure, from the client's perspective, that they don't see any great changes – so they continue to feel safe and they continue to get the good services they did from FACS. We think we did that really well.

There is a lot more focus on running the organisation in a business-like way so that we can make a margin and put that margin back into our organisation. You can't provide the mission if we don't run the organisation at least at a breakeven point.

We are unusual in that we have a very good fundraising capacity and we have generous donors. That allows us to support programs that may not be covered by government.

How can leaders support their employees and maintain quality, given the NDIS pricing?

Rob: I don't think there is any other option. You have to ensure that you have quality services and you have to ensure staff get the right training and ongoing professional development. As I started off by saying, our greatest issue is workforce, so we have to attract, recruit and retain the best people in the sector. It's just something that you cannot afford to cut back on because if you do that it is a downward spiral. You have to get the metrics right on the pricing. It's hard and we are all advocating to the agency. It is just one of those areas we have put our own money into because we felt you can't walk away from that.

I think all organisations can become more efficient. But there are key things you can't walk away from – and quality safeguards and staff development go hand in hand. One of the ways we have done it is through more staff investment not less.

How do you go about hanging onto your good people and attracting the future talent you're going to need for growth?

Rob: We have really increased the people working in our People and Culture division. We have invested in a Workforce Development Plan as part of our strategic workforce plan. We have invested in an Employee Value Exchange so we can promote that externally and also internally about why we are a great place to work.

Frank: Since 2002, CPA has used the Voice Project (founded by Dr Peter Langford at Macquarie University) to independently survey and measure thousands of employees' perceptions. It's been a really good longitudinal study of how we are performing as an organisation.

What was really pleasing were the high results we achieved on questions about change and how we manage change in the last survey in 2018. The Voice Project told us that whatever we've been doing, that we should keep doing it – because it's obviously working!

One of the things that has kept me here for 17 years is the fact that people aren't considered a cost. They are seen as an investment. When you start to use that type of language in an organisation, it puts you in a different frame of mind straight away. You start to look at things in a different, more customer-focused way.

Our commitment to our clients means ensuring that we have the best trained people in the market. For the 2019 financial year the cost of L&D for CPA will be around $5.2 million or 4.2% of payroll per annum. While we still need casual staff, our intention is to build a skilled permanent workforce. This is demonstrated in our staff profile comprising 15% casual and 85% permanent staff (37% permanent full time and 48% permanent part time).

If you can get the right people, in the right roles, supported in the right way, doing the right things, everything else becomes easy. It's a no-brainer, and yet people do it so hard.

Do you offer clear career paths for new people as they come into the organisation?

Frank: One of the first things I did when I came in 2001 was to negotiate two new enterprise awards. I took the opportunity to get rid of a number of things in those enterprise awards that created silos in the organisation. In particular, I was able to get rid of traditional award clauses where people progress based on years of service, rather than performance or competency.

At the same time, I introduced 'Competency-based Role Families' and embedded them into the new enterprise awards. They form the bedrock of our whole HR strategy.

Role families enabled CPA to create career paths across different service streams. At that time the enterprise award was set up in a way that you had different pay rates for the same roles working in different programs, which was absolute madness. Since 2002, if you are a disability support worker, CPA recognises that you have the competencies you need to have – regardless of whether you are working in a lifestyles centre, an accommodation service or respite service.

What is the employee value exchange?

Frank: One of the things that was exposed in the strategic workforce planning we undertook three years ago was that while we have always offered all sorts of benefits to our employees, we had never marketed them effectively internally. Our employees didn't know half the benefits that existed.

In HR land, this is called an employee value proposition (EVP).[16] So we decided to customise it and call it an employee value exchange (EVE), meaning that it's not a one-way street. We provide the benefits and in return we need your 110% commitment to the role. We will create an environment for you to be successful and develop your career. We will give you terms and conditions of employment that are as good, if not better than most places in the NFP sector (and in some cases, better than the commercial sector), but in return we need you to be totally committed to our mission and deliver on the outcomes. It's been a tremendous success.

We have hardly introduced anything new, it was basically raising awareness among our employees about what we have on offer and it's been amazing. People go, 'Wow this is fantastic!', and we say, 'Well actually, we have had the benefit(s) for 10 years.' … 'Really, have you??!!'

The leading (and new) benefit that we used to launch the EVE last April was a very simple, straightforward $100 reimbursement for a health and wellness product or service. So we said, 'Spend $100 before June 30 on a health and wellness initiative for you personally and we will reimburse you. Then as July 1st is the new financial year, you can spend another $100.' That was $200 in the calendar year. The reaction was phenomenal. It's the best value for money we have ever had.

---

16   More information on CPA's Employee Value Exchange can be found in the 'Workplace Culture & the NDIS Workbook' available for download at www.fcmarketing.com.au.

I am interested in how organisations bring their brand alive on a daily basis. How do you do that at CPA?

Frank: It always starts with the management and leadership roles. There is no point beating up the people at the frontline. You've got to start with your management team. The approach is simply that everything has to be value based. No excuses, no compromises, it has to be value based. So that when a team member comes into work every day, they see CPA in action through their team leader and supervisor. There is no other way of doing it. If you get the right people in those roles, modelling the right behaviour, the right culture starts to happen in the workplace.

I am particularly interested in the first three to six months of a new employee's experience. Is there an overarching process for how the induction is structured?

Frank: We are in the throes of reviewing that whole piece right now. Because they are our largest cohort, we have started with the Disability Support Practitioners. We have invested a lot of time and money in that first six months. Not surprisingly, we are finding things that we probably are not doing as well as we should.

Everyone starts at corporate orientation. We have a full day where every person gets to meet the senior leadership team. Then there is a combination of online and face-to-face training programs, totalling around five full days of training that everyone goes through. For our Disability Support Practitioners there are also buddy shifts. This is one of the things that we want to formalise and standardise because we've found from our research that it's a really powerful training tool. If you get the right person in there, shoulder to shoulder, with the new Disability Support Practitioner we can start developing some really good habits from the get-go.

Rob, did you have anything else that you wanted to add?

I am a strong believer in having a very strong ecosystem of services, of all services, not just CPA services. The strength of that network working together can solve some of these problems. Things like workforce won't be solved by one organisation. It has to be looked at and solved by a really strong ecosystem of providers, government and the NDIA. It really needs to be solved holistically rather than piecemeal, otherwise we are all just taking a piece from each other. With the competing needs of health and age care there is this huge need out there for us to work together.

But even to just support people with disability properly you need a really good ecosystem. Families will want the best services close to home at the right price. If we might not be able to provide that, how do we support other organisations to do that? I think that sometimes surprises people in the agency when I say that. But if you go back to my starting point of why did we all start these organisa-tions? It was to do the right thing and to get the right services to people who were not receiving those services. The NDIS was some-thing that we all fought really hard for. It's here now, so how do you make it function, and evolve, and shape it in a way that is going to work for people? There are some great stories out there ... some great achievements have been made.

Chapter 3 ▶

A marketer's approach to culture change

'Clients do not come first. Employees come first. If you take care of your employees, they will take care of the clients.'

Richard Branson

What *is* culture?

There is a mountain of literature about workplace culture. Type the term into your favourite search engine and the pages go on forever.

But what actually *is* workplace culture? I always prefer to use the simplest, most practical definition for things because too often jargon gets in the way of meaning. The definition I like to use for culture is not mine (I'm not sure who first said it), but it is simply:

'How we do things around here.'

It's about daily actions and behaviours.

A marketer's approach

As a marketer, when you dig a little deeper into this it gets really, really interesting. You begin to see that every action and interaction sends a message about what matters. You begin to see the shared values and how the daily behaviours of individuals influence each other to form the actual daily 'patterns of behaviour' of teams.

The non-profit workplace has looked to the corporate environment for so many systems and practices, but very few of these processes translate easily to the non-profit environment. Too often, people overcomplicate workplace culture in the same way they overcomplicate marketing.

I spent 14 years in the corporate sector prior to working with non-profits. In my experience, when it comes to building a healthy culture in a non-profit workplace, corporate language and change management processes can inflict a significant human and financial cost without achieving the desired result. As a marketer I started thinking about how the methodology that I was successfully using to help organisations deliver cost-effective marketing campaigns could also be used to drive staff engagement and positive cultural change. For me, everyone falls into a 'target market'. And every target market includes people with problems and unmet needs. So let's see how a marketer would develop an effective approach to improving workplace culture.

Your two key target markets

In 2017, it occurred to me that the two key target markets which would have the greatest impact on the culture and future sustainability of a disability organisation were the same two groups that were most often overlooked or ignored.

As a first-time author, a funny thing happened that allowed me to test this theory. (Never trust a marketer who does not provide actual market research to substantiate a new strategy.) People I'd never met, who had read my book, started inviting me to speak to their staff, to their boards, to their leadership teams. At every speaking opportunity I decided I would ask the question, 'What do you think are the *two* most important target markets for your financial sustainability?' Nine times out of ten, the response was 'new clients' or 'new participants' – and nothing else except puzzled looks. Over the following 12 months I found that most people could not name the two key target markets. And most people who thought they could name one were actually getting it wrong.

Because they were not aware of the two key target markets, they could not address them as they needed to be addressed in order to have their message heard.

Because demand so outstrips this sector's capacity to supply, the number one marketing priority should be to focus on just two key markets:

- existing staff

- existing customers.

Sustainability is a long-term game not a short-term fix. Across NSW from 2016 to 2018 there was a massive, almost obsessive scramble for new NDIS participants at the expense of existing customers and staff. The disability sector quickly became a very noisy, cluttered market of relatively homogenous mainstream marketing tactics and messages across billboards, TV, websites, social media, doctors' waiting rooms and expos.

The end result? An increasingly anxious and confused customer, high staff turnover and a lot of money wasted on mainstream marketing tactics. And the typical frontline support worker became increasingly stressed and worried about their own job security.

Marketing and HR must work as one

If you are willing to accept that your existing team are a key target market, you can begin to apply basic marketing principles to engage them. You can begin to use one of the most underutilised tools in this sector – the internal brand – to develop an authentic, inside-out, values-driven approach to cultural change.

This approach requires that your marketing and human resources (HR) teams work as one team. Only total collaboration will ensure consistent, top-down, inside-out cultural change.

As we saw in the 'two pyramid' diagram, the new key relationship is the one your frontline staff member has with your customer. As a result, we need to see the customer experience and the employee experience as two sides of the single most important relationship in the organisation. The 'employee value proposition' must mirror the 'customer value proposition', otherwise how can you possibly walk the talk?

It also makes good sense because the employee experience determines the customer experience. Combining the workforce management and customer management functions reinforces a whole-of-organisation approach to effective culture change.

What do employees want?

Daniel Pink, in his book *Drive: The surprising truth about what motivates us*, suggests that there are typically three key intrinsic motivators for employee engagement: autonomy, mastery and purpose.

> 'The most deeply motivated people – not to mention those who are most productive and satisfied – hitch their desires to a cause larger than themselves.'
>
> **Daniel Pink**

I have had the privilege to witness this passion firsthand time and time again in frontline disability support workers. There are literally thousands of 'heroes' out there who are passionate about making a difference on a daily basis.

Chances are you've also seen employees who have lost their passion, or who may never have had it in the first place. From anecdotal and firsthand evidence, this is my own list of what your employees might want:

- to feel supported, to feel heard and to feel that they belong

- enough hours for a decent wage

- to understand the mission and know their contributions matter

- visible leadership

- clear role expectations and performance measures.

The 5-Step Framework

I've developed a practical 5-step approach for any non-profit leader keen to drive a positive, values-based culture throughout their organisation. It's not for academics or corporate change management experts. I'm sure there are even academic theories of change management that contradict my approach. The difference, however, is that this approach was developed in the real world – and it *works*.

Great culture is why wonderful NGOs such as Charity:Water, Fighting Chance and Médecins Sans Frontières have no trouble recruiting the high-quality talent they need. When every staff member feels their own personal values are aligned with the values of the organisation then amazing things can happen. There is a magic that occurs when people truly believe in the organisation they work for. They bring their best selves to work. That's why I call my framework 'Bringing Your Brand Alive'. It's a marketer's approach to culture change that puts people and purpose before process.

High-performance cultures are values-driven. As a result, if your goal is to build a strong culture, you have to first build personal 'ownership' of your brand and the values it stands for. This is what we call in marketing the 'internal brand'. The role of the internal brand is to build team alignment and personal ownership of your mission. The internal brand is built on *trust*.

My framework results in a Culture Action Plan that is built on the principle that your employees have to trust you before your customers ever will. Or as Simon Sinek says:

'Customers will never love a company until the employees love it first.'

An effective Culture Action Plan is one that connects those brand values to individual actions and behaviours that are collectively 'lived' on a daily basis.

My framework is a highly practical, step-by-step guide to help organisations hang onto their great staff, attract the talent they need, support their teams through this perfect storm, and build a high-performance culture under the NDIS.

As in my previous book, this is a model that uses the brand as the 'emotional glue' that binds the organisation internally and externally to the stakeholders you need to survive transformational change.

The following diagram outlines the five steps that we will cover throughout the rest of this book.

Step 1	*Lead with Vision, Purpose and Integrity*
Step 2	*Build your Internal Brand*
Step 3	*Recruit for Values*
Step 4	*Understand your Current Culture*
Step 5	*Create your Culture Action Plan*

Summary

▶ Culture is often defined as *'how we do things around here'*.

▶ Invisible cultural patterns drive actual daily behaviours.

▶ We need to identify the patterns before we can address them.

▶ The two key target markets are existing staff and customers.

▶ The employee experience and the customer experience are two sides of the one key relationship.

▶ A marketing approach to cultural change puts people and purpose before processes.

Interview

Laura O'Reilly, CEO, Fighting Chance

Distressed by the lack of post-school opportunities available for their brother, siblings Laura and Jordan O'Reilly launched Fighting Chance in 2011. The organisation designs, builds and scales social enterprises that provide opportunities for young people with significant disabilities. Today, Fighting Chance is experiencing 'hyper-growth', doubling its turnover every year for the last three years. They run two separate social enterprises, Avenue and Jigsaw. Avenue is a co-working space which exists to rethink the opportunities afforded to young adults with disability. Jigsaw provides digitisation services to corporate and government, to create award-paying jobs, training and pathways to mainstream employment.

Laura, in the three years since our last book interview, how has the NDIS impacted your employees and workforce culture?

There's been a lot of change and not much change as well. As you may recall we were never a block-funded provider, and therefore were operating in an NDIS-like structure pre-NDIS, in so much as we harnessed a casualised workforce, we were already matching staff in line with support hours and we already had a really person-centred culture.

So we were already about 80% there when the NDIS started. I've seen the changes other organisations have gone through and I can't imagine how traumatic it must be for staff who were used to a much more structured service model, based around the convenience of staff themselves.

Where we have seen change is around becoming even more individualised. In the old system, even though we were quite flexible, we were still playing within quite rigid boundaries. The NDIS has really allowed us to open that up in a big way. Now if someone on our team has an idea about what they would like to do to support someone with their goals, we're able to say, go for it! It's been a really positive thing for our staff to have that freedom.

The negative changes have been around our hyper growth. We've doubled our growth every year since I last spoke to you. It's been a bit of a poison chalice. Going from a turnover of $1.5 million to approximately $13 million this year has been a lot for staff to manage. We've had to have a really resilient staff team and a really strong culture to support people through that level of change.

The other negatives have been around the administration side of the NDIS. In my opinion they impose a challenging administrative burden which definitely puts pressure on organisations. Rapid and unpredictable change to processes also puts a lot of strain on staff.

Overall, people understand that it's all for a great cause – we remain passionate believers in the NDIS reform at Fighting Chance. So if we can ride through these growing pains then ultimately we can support our people better.

How do you attract new staff and ensure your new team members are a 'values fit' for your organisation? Is there a 'typical' recruitment and induction process at Fighting Chance?

Overwhelmingly, we attract new staff because they are referred to us by a friend or family member who already works for us. For me, the secret is being values led and being really visible about that; being clear on what we are trying to achieve and empowering our staff to be part of that. Then it's not too hard to find people. A lot of people come in and say, 'I saw your YouTube videos, I love what you guys are doing and what you stand for,' and that's the introduction to the interview.

In terms of induction, historically I would have spent time with people, but with a bigger team now that is increasingly difficult. So we've hired a training manager and introduced a Learning Management System, to house induction videos about our values, what we believe in, what we're trying to achieve and why we started. So we're using technology to bridge that gap.

Typically, we don't hire people with any formal disability qualification or experience. None of our recent senior hires came from the disability sector. Yet many have the lived experience of a child or family member with disability and they bring an array of skills from a range of different industries. I think that's critical to being able to continue to do things differently.

The people we hire bring the 'best in class' aspects of what they've seen in their own industry and we build on that. Very often people are prepared to take a pay cut and work more hours – because they care. They don't have to have lived experience but it's amazing how many people do.

How important is your origin story to your culture?

The origin story is our culture. Storytelling – and the origin story in particular – is the most important tool in our armoury. We also empower others to tell *their* origin story. Why did they say 'yes' to working with Fighting Chance? Why are they here?

Last year we took over management of a new service, with 14 staff joining us in a very short space of time. On the Friday night before they started I invited them all in here. We had some drinks and just sat around and talked about why we're here, why we care about this sector and what we believe in – and it was so powerful! Since then, that group has been bending over backwards and I think it's because they had that initial session to connect with each other, with our story and with Fighting Chance. I talked about why we care and why I care and why I'm asking them to do things in terms of their work. I located it in my brother's experiences and why what they're doing matters.

What role do you play as CEO in creating the inspirational culture at Fighting Chance?

We've had a massive recruitment drive in the last year, with more than 100 staff joining us in that period. We've grown quickly and I've realised that I'm never going to have the chance to do what I did in the old days – to sit with each individual person and talk to them. I now understand that my job is to be telling the origin story and communicating to staff – through team meetings, video, through our induction process and through our LMS system.

If they know what they're meant to be doing from a values perspective then they're going to do it. If they don't understand the point of what they're being asked to do then it's not possible for them to nail it.

I need to go from 10% of my time on that stuff to spending 90% of my time talking with staff. It's an interesting challenge for me because I'm an introvert. But it's really critical that I do it.

In our last interview you mentioned that you hoped to do more work articulating your brand and culture. How has this developed? What role do your brand values 'Excellence, The Power of Yes and Flexibility' play in driving your high-performance culture?

Brand has been a big focus for Fighting Chance since the roll out of the NDIS commenced. We've rebranded Fighting Chance and Avenue, and are in the process of rebranding Jigsaw, and have been able to drill into the core message of what we're trying to achieve. For Fighting Chance the new tagline is *What if* and for Avenue it's *For All*. The values are still the same but we've been able to articulate them in a slightly different way with new visuals and all the collateral around that.

We've also just implemented a values-led strategic planning program across the organisation. It asks every individual to articulate what their personal values were and then every team, and that all feeds into the broader Fighting Chance values. Those three values you mentioned are still at the top of our list and now we better reflect that through the clarity created by a strong brand.

You run a few social enterprises; how would you describe your workplace culture and how do your business model(s) support it?

We take a very commercial approach to the enterprises that we build. They have to be sustainable, efficient and practical. They have to solve a problem; they have to achieve something.

That reflects our culture. Our staff like working like that. We encourage innovation. We encourage people to fix things that aren't working and adopt a customer service approach because we haven't got big government grants to fall back on. We have to deliver services that our customers love and will want to purchase again. That all drives our culture in a big way.

We've adopted a decentralised approach but with efficiency at the heart of it. Fighting Chance is at the centre of the model with the mission of coming up with ideas and providing a central suite of support services such as finance, communications and marketing, site rollout and technology. It's the heart of the business. Then around that we have our enterprises, Avenue and Jigsaw, each with their own organisational structure, vision, mission and goals. That gives you the best of both worlds – efficiency of scale in key administrative functions, coupled with lean, focused structures driving the enterprises forward.

What do you think are the biggest challenges facing the disability sector now? If you had one key message for disability service providers right now, what would it be?

It's still the same thing that I have been saying since the NDIS began its national roll out in 2016. I understand that it's really hard to redesign programs but I think providers need to get more focused on the quality of frontline services: What are the models? Are we differentiated enough? Are we really, truly empowering people to meet their goals? That should be 80% of the conversation.

A lot of providers are too focused on structure or governance or back-of-house issues – which are still important issues – but I still don't see them innovating in terms of actual service delivery.

To be honest they're all related. Let's take the piece we've been talking about today, the staff team. If you do the best induction with an inspiring origin story and then you ask staff to deliver a program that does not align with the origin story – it's pointless.

As a sector we need to get really focused on the quality of services we're delivering. Not just the quality, but the innovation at the heart of services, the differentiation within the sector. If you do that then people will want to work for you, families are happy, it goes a long way towards achieving staff retention and a strong brand. We need to start innovating in a much bigger way than we're doing.

There is cool stuff starting to emerge. Little things are popping up everywhere at the grassroots level which is really exciting. I think that over the next 20 years the sector will go from being a handful of massive providers to thousands of little providers all doing unique models of service exceptionally well. When that happens, people with disability will genuinely have choice and control over their supports.

Interview

Leanne Fretten, CEO, Sylvanvale Foundation

Sylvanvale Foundation, formerly the Handicapped Children's Centre of New South Wales, was founded in 1947 when a group of parents united to form an organisation that would give their children with a disability a better quality of life through access to education and social inclusion. It now has 660 staff supporting over 750 children and adults across 50 locations in southern and western Sydney. Leanne first joined Sylvanvale as an Occupational Therapist in 2004. She has since held various management roles across a number of departments including Children's Services, Client Services and People & Culture. She was promoted to Chief Executive Officer in 2016.

Leanne, what do you think are the key challenges facing the disability sector right now? If you had a key message for other providers what would it be?

There are so many challenges. That's part of the issue. One of the big emerging issues for us is access to a capable and talented workforce. It has shifted right up our priority listing.

Obviously the regulated pricing and, in my opinion, the incorrect assumptions that underpin the agency's pricing methodology. That now coupled with the requirements of the quality and safe guarding commission (the NDIS Commission). I feel that they are often in direct conflict with one another.

As a concrete example, we have requirements to report restrictive practices including those authorised and unauthorised. One of those requirements of authorisation is that you have a current behaviour support plan in place where a participant has restrictive practices. But what if the NDIA does not fund the participant to have a behaviour support plan? We are in breach of the regulations around restrictive practices and are required to report ourselves for unauthorised use of a restrictive practice, because behaviour support isn't funded in a plan.

To get that changed means a plan review. It can take up to nine months, and in the interim we are in breach of the regulation, reporting ourselves to the commission. So, there are some administrative and logistical issues there that we are doing unfunded.

The other major challenge is managing cashflow. With the perennial offs and ons of plans we are having to manage our funds really tightly. We have to manage our cash week to week, ensuring we have enough working capital to pay our obligations as and when they fall due.

I recall you saying to me a year ago that the NDIA owed you $7 million stretching back almost a year; was that correct?

We had large amounts of funds outstanding late last year but the majority of that was paid in November and December. This is an ongoing issue for all NDIS participants, but has been particularly problematic for those participants accessing Supported Independent Living (SIL) services which are NDIA managed. For some of our participants it has been months in between plans. In that period where no plan exists we continue to provide the service even though we are not being paid by the agency. We have an obligation to the people we support to provide continuity of service. That is an ongoing administrative cost to chase the funds and also a loss of revenue from the interest lost as our reserves are being spent on providing services, while we await payments. At a time when we should be trying to shrink our overheads and be more efficient, we are actually doing the opposite and having to put extra people on to chase payments. In essence we are providing financing for the Federal Government with no compensation for this loss of revenue.

I think the other thing that is a big challenge is keeping up with the external policy environment as it is changing so rapidly. As an example, new prices were released in mid-February, with the implementation being effective prior to that on the first of February. So you are often playing catch up and our peak bodies are also struggling to be ahead of the game as the communication and relationship management from the agency is sporadic. You have to have staff and resources that constantly keep pace with all these changes.

So, in terms of the key message for other disability providers?

In terms of the key message, it's that you have to continue to be agile. I don't think that it is going to slow down or change. I also feel that as a CEO you actually need to know your business inside and out. You need to continue to work *in* the business and *on it* – and get that balance right.

You need to know your business intimately and you need to surround yourself, as a CEO, with good people. I see that as really critical going forward. You need to have people who are agile and can work in such a fast-paced change environment.

In terms of attracting the talent you need, are you looking outside the sector?

For my executive team, I went to market looking for specific skillsets that we didn't have in the sector so we have brought people into the business who have come from outside the sector. They have brought particular skills but they also have the values alignment.

At the frontline we have been working really hard on values-based recruitment for support worker recruitment. Basically, everyone participates in a group interview. Then there are group exercises around our five values to identify people who are potentially misaligned with the organisation's values before they are hired.

We have taken the approach that we can teach the skills but we are recruiting for organisational fit and values. This has certainly opened up the talent pool a little bit wider and we are also now tracking the tenure of those new recruits.

In line with that, we have expanded our induction process to a five-day induction across all of those new starters. We have had to align that to the new quality and safeguarding requirements as well. So, we are investing heavily up front, to ensure the people are skilled and ready for when they hit the frontline, which is great.

I think the other thing that we are looking at in terms of future talent is retaining those that we already have in the business. Especially our frontline staff and managers. It is so easy to go and get another job. Remuneration is one lever to retain talent, but more often people are looking for a career path, personal development and flexibility around work/life balance.

How do you find the connection between your frontline, your middle management and your administration teams?

We restructured our business early 2018 and we have tried to centralise as many administration functions as we can. We have centralised rostering, the management of our service agreements and our plan review processes to lighten the load of the frontline managers. You can have the best head office team ever but unless they are empowering the frontline team it will all fall over.

We are trying as much as possible to remove the paperwork so that they can be forward facing, focusing on participants and their frontline teams.

We also reduced the span of control. At one point we had a ratio of about 1:15 or so manager to staff member; that is now down to about 1:10 ratio. At a time when other organisations are stripping management out, we have made a decision to invest in the management at the frontline.

How important is the culture at Sylvanvale? How do you keep your values front of mind for you?

I think culture is something that's really difficult because it is abstract, but I liken it to *your heart and your soul,* and I think that is what makes Sylvanvale special and will differentiate us in the marketplace. So, I think it is critical.

We have been doing a lot of work on keeping our values front and centre. I talk to every new group of inductees on the first day about our values. I give them concrete examples of what I mean by those values to make it real so that they are not simply words on a page.

In every site we have our values posters, so they are front and centre and we have tried to use a bit of humour as well. For example, we have a poster (that the marketing team despise actually) I call the *values in action* poster and so it will list one of our values and then it will link to a specific behaviour.

Performance management is the next step, but I have to say we are not really that far down the path with that yet.

I remember Cathy Quinn, your Operations Manager, saying that the frontline is now head office's customer.

Yes, we use that language. Different head office teams respond differently and that is a work in progress!

I talk at induction about our three strategic pillars and I often say that the sustainability pillar (which is all about the dollars) is for me and head office to worry about. The frontline delivers on our customer service pillar and our quality pillar. If we get those two things right, sustainability will come.

The other thing that we have done is tighten up our change management processes to cope with the amount of change. I am trying to ensure that we don't bombard the frontline team with change requests. It's too easy to just push things out to the frontline without any prior thought.

How does your brand support your culture?

We rebranded a couple of years ago now and I think the brand itself does align with our history. We have bright colours that all do link in some way to our values, and we talk in induction about that to our staff. So, there is a lot of theory of how the brand links to culture. But have we made it really come alive? I think we still have work to do there. I think it is still a culture of sub-cultures. You often find that within big organisations, so yes, we still have work to do.

On a practical daily basis, how has your role changed from what the previous CEO's might have been?

I can tell you where each of our SIL participants is currently up to in the plan review cycle, who has been quoted and where it is up to. I would have said 12 months ago that the CEO should not have to know that. Now because of the amount of change I think it's important that you know your business intimately.

I think in terms of driving culture it is crucial to be walking the talk. One of our values is Respect, so this month I am driving *timeliness* with my executive team and *that it is disrespectful of people's time to show up for meetings late*. We have to set the example with that. We also have to be *available* and *present*.

I take a real interest in my staff and what projects they are working on. I make an effort to walk the floor and talk to people. It is not tokenistic. I think you have to actually genuinely engage. I can see them thinking, '*Oh she does know!*' Yes I do know, and I am interested in how it is going and if I need to pull any levers to assist the project to meet its deliverable within the timelines.

Change is just business as usual now. That is just the environment we are in. This year is our *year of engagement*. That is our new buzzword. Engage. Engage. Engage. Customers and staff. So in everything we do.

Chapter 4 ▶

Step 1: Lead with Vision, Purpose and Integrity

'The role of CEO is critical; it needs to drive the culture and communicate the vision. It has to come from the top down; they need to see
me leading by example. I think the culture and the vision is the *collective soul of an organisation*.'

Melinda Kubisa, CEO, Community Living Options SA

In the Royal Commission into Australia's financial institutions last
year we were shown what happens when processes take over from
human transparency and effective oversight. The dogged pursuit
of 'vertical integration' led to a conflict of interest that failed the
best interests of customers. Poor cultural practices, corruption, self-
interest and impenetrable bureaucracies flooded in to fill the leadership vacuum.

Looking over all the case studies and interviews I've prepared
for this book, it occurred to me that there was one single game-
changing ingredient that, if removed, leads to cultural collapse:
integrity of leadership.

Working closely with CEOs in the not-for-profit sector over the
last 20 years, I've seen firsthand the direct correlation between cultural health and the integrity of leadership, and I've come to believe
that the two are inseparable.

Let's take a look …

Cultural health and language

A key indicator of culture is the language we use. Somewhere along the way, words like *kindness, compassion* and *integrity* left the leadership conversation and were replaced with words like *metrics, change management, agile* and *analytics*.

It becomes easy to forget that we're talking about actual people who breathe, feel and live. It becomes even easier to forget that organisations only work if we can engage the hearts and minds of the people who work there. Not human 'resources', but 'humans'.

In a values-driven organisation, the business is underpinned by its values which serve as guiding criteria for daily actions and decision making.

Effective leadership is about providing clarity of direction and measuring performance within an environment that enables employees to personally identify with the organisation's values and purpose. It's the tone at the top that sets the culture. Everything else flows from there.

A strong culture requires integrity of leadership.

The CEO and board relationship

In the Australian disability sector the role of the CEO has never been under more pressure. It's not surprising that in the last 12 months we have seen so many CEOs retiring early, or in some cases being forcibly removed by their boards who failed to get their heads around the scale of the change agenda.

The CEO of a $70 million organisation recently shared with me his relief that 'at least he had one board member who really understood' what he was facing because he was also a CEO in the sector.

Otherwise, he said, 'I would have been well and truly sacked by now!'

Too often boards have failed to come to grips with the scale of change required by the NDIS. Or worse, the board fails to devote the time and energy required to understand the new operating environment. As a result, the CEO must 'educate up' as well as 'educate down', and lacks the professional support they need to drive the operational and transformational changes required for sustainability.

I've presented to boards who believed that the right level of investment in the right technology would be sufficient to prepare their organisation for the NDIS. This is no different to thinking that a Porsche without petrol will help you escape a firestorm.

I've run workshops that were attended by long-serving directors who had never actually visited the sites of service delivery, or were meeting long-serving senior leadership team members for the first time at my workshop.

In my experience, strong leadership in this sector is only possible when the CEO has the full support of their chairperson and board. A healthy, robust culture depends on it.

I've seen how boards directly influence the culture of an organisation. The work on culture is never 'completed'. It requires ongoing monitoring of the right early indicators.

Does *your* board walk the talk? Do they know what questions to ask and what indicators to monitor? Are they mobilised into committees with clear reporting deadlines? How well informed are they of the changing landscape? Do they express interest in how your values work in practice? Do they regularly refer to the organisation's mission and values as their decision-making criteria?[17]

---

17 For an excellent summary of the governance and culture lessons from the Hayne Report for the NFP sector visit: https://probonoaustralia.com.au/news/2019/06/sponsoredcontent-lessons-from-the-banking-royal-commission-for-the-nfp-sector/.

Board composition and the NDIS

Most important of all, the NDIS transformation requires a *new type of board.*

Traditionally, disability providers were established by parents keen to ensure their children had the opportunities they deserved. It's even more critical now that people with a lived experience of disability are on every organisation's board and supported to participate fully.

From the interviews in this book, it's clear that board composition is changing across the sector as organisations seek out new skills, networks and commercial experience. However, this only works if the new directors are also a genuine culture fit.

Nicola Hayhoe, CEO of The Housing Connection, commented:

> **Having new directors or new boards can be a real tipping point, or it has been in the past. It can be seen as a real risk for our culture. It's my role to make sure there is alignment for our mission, purpose and values at the board level and that this translates into strategic planning which translates into operational planning. Having that framework to carry through the organisation in everything we do.**

The NDIS transformation requires directors with new skillsets and experience such as technology, finance, communications and marketing. Less obvious, but just as important, are directors who understand how to run a successful small business – people who are natural salespeople, natural 'community connectors', natural partnership builders who are deeply committed to serving the mission.

As mentioned previously, disability is a local business. Whether you're a statewide organisation or operating in one locality only, you need to think and act as if you're running a local business serving the local needs in each local community. Successful small businesses are built on local trust. The most successful small business owners naturally think in terms of local partnerships, they decentralise the decision making into local hubs, and they understand that the closer they are to the community they serve, the more they will be trusted.

The role of the Vision

I often find that people get confused about the difference between a Vision and a Mission.

A Vision is simply a destination statement. When your team feels connected to your Vision, it creates a synergy, an energy of its own that helps you align the organisation and actually create the future.

A strong Vision is:

- clear and visible with future-tense verbs

- bold and inspirational

- memorable

- concise.

As mentioned in my previous book, one of my favourite Vision statements is Bill Gates's original for Microsoft: 'A computer on every desk and in every home'.

I've seen directors roll their eyes when I've suggested that the flowery statement at the top of their strategic plan is too vague to provide their team with any clear sense of direction. Vision statements can't be just token words on a page. Nor should they be tested and crafted letter by letter until they've lost their passion or meaning.

This is not about playing with words. It's about laying strong foundations. Vision clarity is an essential prerequisite for a strong organisational culture. (If you're struggling with culture, it's highly unlikely that anyone in your organisation can repeat your Vision statement.)

If your organisation has a Vision that sounds more like a motherhood statement, add some sentences beneath it that unpack what that Vision actually looks like. Because every employee in your organisation needs to be able to 'own the Vision' and feel that they can play a role in achieving it. How can you possibly encourage innovation if only the CEO and board know the end game? As I wrote in my previous book, a shared Vision is owned by everyone in the organisation. Command and control leadership won't get you to sustainability.

The role of the Mission

The Mission describes *why* you exist, your reason for being. There is still a lot of confusion about the role of the Mission – and this stuff really matters if you're seeking positive culture change. Because, once again, everyone has to 'own' the Mission. As Simon Sinek writes in his groundbreaking book *Start with Why*:[18]

> **If the leader of the organisation can't clearly articulate why the organisation exists in terms beyond its products or services then how does he expect the employees to know why to come to work?**

If your board spends more time focusing on 'how will we survive?' than 'how can we serve?' then you know you're looking at organisational 'mission drift'. Your Mission has lost relevance to the individuals and families it was created to serve.

Without relevance there is no passion, there is no connection, there is no mission. Your employees want to know that their work is

---

18   S.Sinek, *Start with Why*, Portfolio Penguin, 2009.

meaningful, that their contribution matters, that it aligns with their values. Mission relevance is a fundamental prerequisite for a strong culture.

As Elise Taylor, GM Strategy & Development for Cerebral Palsy Alliance, shares in her interview:

> **Culturally, having that mission clarity is very important. That is the tight rope: making sure that you are living to your core values. Our mission and our vision are the things we have to keep going back to. Right now it is really important.**

Time and again, this same point was made in the interviews for this book. For Kerry Stubbs, CEO and Managing Director of Northcott, it was her key message for providers:

> **I think my key message for providers would be that now is the time to refocus on your purpose as an organisation. What's the reason you exist? What is your mission? Are you making sure that whatever you do in these turbulent times that you are still focusing on your mission? If you can't deliver services sustainably, then perhaps it's time to consider doing something else.**

The role of the origin story

'What must be always preserved is the spirit of the work; its life will depend on the generations that transmit this spirit and bring it to life.'

Antonio Gaudi on the crowning achievement of his life's work, the Sagrada Familia

Some time ago I was invited to prepare a strategic marketing plan for a disability service provider. The organisation was experiencing significant change fatigue and lacked any sense of connection across their many sites and services.

Perhaps the first, really telling indicator was that of all the people I interviewed at the start of the contract, only two could tell me their organisation's origin story with any passion in their voice. Only two people could explain how and why the organisation began, the need they were responding to all those years ago, and how today they continue to find new, exciting ways to meet the changing needs of the people they serve. Only two people were 'on a mission', the rest 'knew that the organisation had a mission statement'.

In my Culture Masterclass I now ask the question: 'What do you think is the single most powerful story for building your culture?' It's the organisation's origin story; the who, why and how that led to your existence.

Few so far have nailed it. I've seen it with my own eyes. Having worked with large and small providers now in most states of Australia, I've seen how this simple story connects teams. It connects your past to your future. It connects your employees to your purpose. It demonstrates that you are still true to your cause and finding new relevance for your mission.

Last year, I had the pleasure of working with a wonderful organisation in Gympie, Queensland named Bravo Disability Support Network. I had the privilege of sitting around the table with the founders, who are still directors. At every AGM, they read out their origin story so that they never lose touch with their 'why'. It's no surprise that they have a fantastic, vibrant workplace culture.

If all you do in your organisation is learn how to tell and share your origin story, things will begin to shift. And don't just tell the story, share the images, create awards in memory of your founders, do whatever you need to do to show you are holding true to your purpose; that your organisation is still relevant. It demonstrates that you walk the talk. It demonstrates that you can be trusted.

One of the most moving, most authentic origin stories I've heard belongs to Fighting Chance. This organisation really understands the power of simple storytelling and how to structure its stories. It comes as no surprise that they have no problem with recruitment. (See my interview with CEO Laura O'Reilly on page 70). Not everyone will have an immediate family member at the heart of their origin story, but your founders probably would have, so tell it from their point of view.

The layer most at risk

'I think we have only two or three people who are feeling really negative.'

This was the quiet 'heads up' from the CEO of a disability organisation I received on the morning before our first workshop. But in the week prior I had interviewed the 24 attendees one on one, and I knew that his *entire middle management layer* was at a professional breaking point. It was not surprising that some of them failed to show.

If you *think you might have* a culture problem, in my experience it's actually likely to be far more widespread than you believe. Because, chances are, you may not be reading the signs (or monitoring the right indicators).

For this provider, the issue wasn't that his middle management were feeling negative – they were feeling completely ignored. The fact that he had no idea about this only confirms that feeling. In our confidential interviews, the feelings expressed by these managers felt like there was actually no hope of support. They were being crunched on both sides. They felt frustrated and overwhelmed by the administrative burden, the expectations on them from above, and the push back they were receiving from their frontline staff.

Time and again, the management layer I see most at risk of burnout and culture failure is the frontline team leaders. Depending upon how hierarchical your structure is, you might call it middle management. The more layers of management between the CEO and the frontline, the greater the pressure on the frontline team leaders.

The layer most at risk

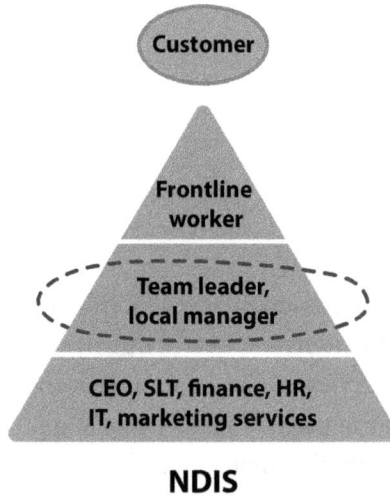

Customer

Frontline worker

Team leader, local manager

CEO, SLT, finance, HR, IT, marketing services

NDIS

Great support workers burn out so much faster than most people because they often give everything they've got to support their customers. People who care this much may also struggle with work/life boundary issues because they are always 'there' for others.

As mentioned earlier, people bring their whole selves to work, not just their work self.

Consider the typical workplace demographics and you begin to understand why there is so much pressure on this layer of management. We know that 76% of the disability workforce is female.

In March 2018, 93% of allied health professionals in this sector were women, but only 21% were aged over 44.[19] However, 44% of support workers are aged 45 or more.[20]

For many, this can set up very real cultural silos between therapists and support workers divided by age, qualifications and life experience. (I keep thinking about how language impacts relationships, and the therapist in chapter 2 who only considered her therapist colleagues to be 'professionals'.)

Women aged 45-plus are often juggling multiple unpaid roles. They may be simultaneously looking after kids, grandkids and elderly parents while juggling more than one job in order to earn enough money from an unpredictable roster. They're often struggling with self-esteem issues because they have no time or funds for themselves.

They need strong support from their team leaders and sensitive performance management or they can quickly burn out.

Your frontline team leaders are the layer most at risk in the current environment. They are also the key to unlocking cultural inertia and driving positive cultural change. Their number one priority must be to support your frontline support workers; you need them performing at a high level. The customer experience depends on it.

Everyone talks about the tone at the top (including me). It may sound like an overreaction, but you not only need to control the tone from the top but, even more urgently, you may need to understand the tone at the middle and provide emergency relief!

Measure what matters

Two months ago I was running a workshop interstate when I heard a phrase that I've now heard over and over again: 'We just had to set culture to one side so we could get everything else done.'

---

19   Australian Disability Workforce Report July 2018.
20   NDS State of the Sector Report December 2018.

Clearly, this particular manager was not required to regularly report on any cultural indicators to her CEO. If she had been responsible for measuring any aspect of it and reporting on that measure regularly, culture would not have been set aside for long.

Most organisations don't monitor cultural indicators on a regular basis. Successful cultural transformation takes at least three years and requires regular monitoring. Existing employee and customer metrics such as staff engagement surveys or Net Promoter Scores (NPS) are lagging indicators.

How does your organisation report on cultural health to your board? Is it simply the annual staff retention figures and staff satisfaction survey? Or have you attempted to develop something more meaningful that can be measured at any point in time and then watched as a trend?

If you're serious about culture change, you need to add in some leading indicators of progress. You need to get more human and more granular. This means looking for the weekly 'human' clues or behaviours that indicate cultural fatigue or decline – and addressing this sooner rather than later.

Some examples are given in the following box, but it's really a matter of understanding and applying the metrics that best suit your organisation. Take a commonsense, human approach around what is an easy, reliable measure of staff engagement in your workplace. (Keep in mind Eric Reis's comment in his book *The Lean Startup*: 'Remember, metrics are people too!')

The old saying 'what gets measured, gets managed' absolutely applies to workplace culture. So, identify the indicators that make the most sense for your organisation and start monitoring them now, rather than waiting another 6 to 12 months until the next engagement survey. Because with the speed of change in the Australian disability sector, 6 to 12 months is a very long time.

New indicators of cultural health

▶ Weekly team meeting attendance rates. (I know this sounds like school, but believe me, so many organisations don't even get their staff attending team meetings. How can you support them – or keep them – if you never see them?)

▶ Weekly or monthly absenteeism rates.

▶ Monthly team social events.

▶ Monthly staff rewards/awards.

▶ Monthly staff retention.

▶ Monthly rate of service cancellations versus services delivered.

▶ The number of CEO site visits.

▶ The number of CEO–frontline team leader face-to-face meetings.

▶ The number of CEO–participant (and family) face-to-face interactions.

▶ The number of cross-functional projects active at any one time.

▶ Board meeting attendance rates.

▶ Positive and negative customer feedback rates.

▶ The number of employees who know your origin story.

▶ Performance incentives are tied to organisational values.

Seven characteristics of great CEOs

This is just my own pick of the top characteristics of great CEOs. There are plenty of living examples of these characteristics in the interviewees for this book:

1. They are authentic, true to themselves and give others permission to be the same. They understand that people bring their whole selves to work, not just their work self.

2. They understand they need to be a listener and a learner. They ask questions of their customers, their ex-customers and every layer of their organisation. They understand that face-to-face communication builds trust and understanding.

3. They know that their competitors are not the benchmark for anything. They think strategically. They know their niche and unique value proposition. They value authentic co-design and seek to redefine the customer experience beyond any previous benchmark or norm.

4. They are humble. They admit mistakes and they make it safe for others to explore new ideas, fail and learn. They create a culture where people are allowed to question the way things have always been done and feel encouraged to suggest improvements. They value transparency and accountability in all processes. They understand that complex environments require patience, persistence and diverse solutions. That sometimes 'fast is slow'.

5. They live and breathe their values; they don't just talk about them. They find ways to personally connect with their employees that reflect the organisation's values.

6. Their employees feel that their opinions matter, their work matters and their personal values are a strong fit with the organisation's culture.

7. They understand that their employees want visible leadership around a clear vision and purpose. This means Vision clarity, Mission clarity, and role clarity. They reward their employees for living the organisation's values; they share and celebrate their success stories often.

Summary

▶ Culture is a top-down process.

▶ Integrity of leadership is essential for cultural health.

▶ The role of CEO has never been under more pressure.

▶ Boards must step up and come to grips with the scale of change required.

▶ A new type of board is needed to support the CEO.

▶ A shared Vision is a destination statement 'owned' by the entire organisation.

▶ A Mission is why you exist; mission relevance is a fundamental prerequisite for a strong culture. The need to survive is not a sufficient purpose to sustain culture.

▶ The origin story is the single most powerful story for building culture.

▶ The management layer most at risk of change fatigue and cultural inertia is the frontline team leaders.

▶ We need new indicators for cultural health.

▶ Great CEOs exhibit similar characteristics.

Interview

Sean Dempsey, CEO, Plan Partners

Plan Partners are one of Australia's largest providers of plan management and support co-ordination services to NDIS participants. The organisation began in 2016, as the joint initiative of Disability Services Australia and McMillan Shakespeare Group to provide independent plan management and support co-ordination services to help people realise the Scheme's potential. Sean Dempsey is the CEO and one of the original founders of the business. He is a 'walk-the-talk' leader with a strong personal commitment to being 'out in front' listening to his customers and his staff.

Sean, what do you think are the biggest challenges facing the sector right now, and if you had a key message for providers what would it be?

I think there are two fundamental areas that are challenging the sector now. The first is that the traditional streams of revenue are completely changing. The disability sector has traditionally relied on government funding or a fundraising arm. Those organisations now need to materially change their approach.

This impacts their entire business, right through to the types of people they employ, their systems, technology and communications and, most importantly, the view they take towards their customers and customer outcomes.

The second challenge falls out of that. The NDIS is now influencing consumer behaviour. Through the NDIS, people with a disability can now make their own choices and control their own funding and supports as any consumer should be able to do.

If they don't like the services they are receiving, they can move away from a service provider, in the same way that anyone else would if they were unhappy with the services they were receiving from their insurance company, their electricity or gas provider. The challenge for all organisations in the disability sector is that they now have to operate in a competitive market, and many have little experience of true competition.

This raises the issue of how do you support the consumer to make an informed decision when really, they have never had choices before?

Support co-ordination is at the heart of that for us. We take a very strong view that support co-ordination is a capacity-building exercise.

We take our role in that very seriously. We talk to customers about the services we're providing all the time, checking back to ensure that they get the support they were looking for. Words like empowerment and enablement, choice and control are fundamental to how we are trying to help our customers achieve their goals in life.

However, although support co-ordination is a capacity-building support, it won't go away. Support co-ordination will be more important as we move into the future rather than less. At least 40% of the NDIS Plans we are seeing now include support co-ordination.

Plan management also plays an important role in this. For a variety of reasons, many participants find it difficult to take full advantage of their funding, leading to unspent funds and the risk of less funding next year. Or they might spend their budgets incorrectly, run out of funding too soon and risk not being able to pay for their services. Plan management enables people to keep track of their funding and make informed choices of which supports they can purchase. It allows them to fully utilise their funding to live the life they want and achieve the goals in their NDIS plan.

It appears that the trend is for participants to either self-manage their NDIS plans or use independent Plan Managers rather than having NDIA manage their funds. What do you think is driving that trend?

I think the NDIA is starting to truly see the value of independent intermediaries and investment from the private sector and the NFP sector, in helping them do some of the heavy lifting the NDIA needs to do and improving the outcomes of the Scheme.

There are many people at senior levels in the NDIA who are embracing our involvement. We have said to everyone who will listen, we can only be successful if we have a successful scheme and a successful agency. That is why 'Making the NDIS a success' is one of the key commitments we have defined in our Customer Charter.

I also think the trend is being driven by the customer. Participants are saying there has got to be a better way of doing this, so they go out and do their research and that leads them to plan management and support co-ordination. So the trend is probably due to both the NDIA and the NDIS participants seeking a better way.

As a commercial operator, how do you address the perceived mission split between 'for-profit' and 'non-profit' organisations?

Any organisation, whether it is private or public, 'for-profit' or 'not-for-profit', must be driven by a strong mission if it is to be successful. It must have an outcome that is customer based and quantifiable in terms of the success of delivering goods, services, and products to its consumers.

The most successful public or private sector organisations have shareholders that expect a return on the investment that they have made; they have a mission at their heart; they have a vision of what they want to be and how they want to get there.

We spend a lot of time and effort talking about where we have come from, about where we are going, about our values and about the mission that we need to hold dear, every minute of every day.

We've got about 75 people working for us now, and with supreme confidence I could say that if you spoke to every single one of them and asked, 'Why did you come to work today?' not one of those people would say they came to work to make money or to help the organisation make money. The people who are driven by *that* outcome are not the people that work at Plan Partners. Instead, they would say

'I'm here to support people to live their best life'. We realise that every customer is different. We realise that every invoice we pay for our customers, has a story behind it. In fact, every invoice we pay means that someone who trusts us is one step closer to to realising their life goals. I cannot over emphasise how important that is for every single member of our team.

So, what is your niche? What is the gap in the market that Plan Partners was built to fill?

Many people feel lost when they receive their NDIS plan. Managing finances and finding the right provider to suit their needs is not easy or straightforward. Our niche is to support people to get the most from their plan. To realise the full potential of their funding so they can focus on living the life they want.

Some people have never experienced a change of this magnitude. Many people are under a greater amount of stress, uncertainty, and anxiety about what the future means. So, we see our niche as being one of guidance and navigation. We help people bring their NDIS plan to life.

Our independence is critical. We guide people to service providers on the basis of their goals and needs, not on the basis of what might be good for our business. There is no money changing hands through receipt or payment for referral of business.

How do you address the issue of attracting new staff? Are you looking for people specifically with disability or social services experience?

Attracting talent to our business is about finding individuals who want to go the extra mile to support people with disability and their carers.

The qualities of the individual are the most important. Whether they come with disability or social services experience or from a commercial background or for-profit or not-for-profit, these are all secondary considerations.

There are many, many different sectors that people who demonstrate that extraordinary affinity for another human being might come from.

There are two qualities we look for:

- They have to have resilience; they must be able to cope with some of the very challenging situations that we find our customers living with, and they must have an enormous dose of emotional intelligence and self-awareness.

- They have to also be a problem solver. We often use the phrase, 'We will be part of the solution and will not allow ourselves to be part of a problem'.

Our people have to be able to say, 'Right. I have been presented with a problem, I am the tenth person to be involved and it is my job at Plan Partners to find a solution for this problem.'

About 90% of the time, the problems that we we deal with have got absolutely nothing to do with us, but with the NDIA, planner or service provider. But our people will move forward and try to solve the problem, because they understand that many of our customers don't know how to solve these issues themselves.

As CEO, how important is culture to you? How do you keep the team up when they might be going through a really tough time?

There is nothing more important than teamwork and the camaraderie that our people show towards each other. Whether it is coaching them to help them work through a problem, whether it's having a laugh or having a chat when you see that someone needs it (e.g. you may have overheard a difficult phone call).

Whatever the issue, we encourage our team to be there for each other.

There is nothing more important than the way our people treat each other on a daily basis; that's the way we do things at Plan Partners.

This comes through in the set of values that we have created:

- We put people first.

- We demonstrate integrity.

- We own it.

- We're one team.

What about remote teams? How do you keep them engaged?

The engagement can be difficult with remote teams; there is no doubt about that. Plan Partners now operates in all states of Australia, with five offices in metropolitan areas and support co-ordinators in more remote areas. Very early on, we set up Skype for everyone, so that no matter whether our people are 1000 or 2000 km apart they can still have a face-to-face conversation. We encourage our people to Skype first.

There are a couple of other things that support that. Our intranet is a hub for all of the information, all of the training, all of the documents, anything that any of our people want. We have a profile of each of our people that is quite interactive. We have built our own platform on Office 365 and we use Yammer as a conversation tool as well.

We also try to get out and see the guys as often as we can. Andrea, our Head of Support Co-ordination, and I were in Albury for the day. So we jumped on a train and spent the day with our team there. We had a bit of a business review but it was more so that I could buy them a cup of tea, a bite to eat at lunch, have a laugh and get out of the office for the day. We also fly people from our other offices down to our office in Melbourne quite regularly.

How do you keep your values front of mind for your team?

We have developed what we're calling our *'Spotted Awards'* based on our values.

These awards are peer-driven nominations that recognise behaviours that demonstrate our values in action. So, if one of our people 'spots' another of their colleagues doing something that is clearly in line with our values, they have a postcard size Spotted Award nomination that they fill in and put up on our Hero Wall or in an online form on our Intranet. One every month we pick a winner of the Spotted Award.

We bought a life-size fluffy dog called Spot that sits on the desk of the Spotted Award Winner for the next month as reinforcement that they won the Spotted Award. The Award has been a huge success. It's fun, it's peer recognition and it's a clear reinforcement of our values.

A lot of CEOs in this space really struggle to get out from behind the desk. What would you say to people who find that really challenging?

I would say: 'Reflect on what your role as CEO is really about.'

I could say, with no hesitation, that an hour of my time spent talking with three of my people about their day, about their customers, is going to return so much more than answering 20 emails. There is just no doubt about that. The bottom line is that 20 minutes spent with Emily, one of our Customer Service Officers, is going to produce a far greater pay off than 20 minutes answering five emails from my directors or whoever else it might be.

If you find it really challenging to get out from behind the desk the answer might to get yourself a GM if your financials allow for that. Or it might be to empower some of the other people that you have got working with you to do some of that. It might also be to leave that stuff until people start to go home and work another couple of hours. So, the answer is probably unique to everyone's situation.

Interview

David Moody, Acting Chief Executive Officer, National Disability Services

David Moody is the Acting Chief Executive Officer of National Disability Services (NDS), Australia's peak industry body for non-government disability services. David's career history has seen him working as a lawyer and partner at a leading personal injuries law firm and leading teams in the Victorian Public Service responsible for national health and safety reform, strategic OHS policy, OHS legislation and regulations and regulatory framework development, budget strategy and corporate planning and leading the team responsible for co-ordinating the Victorian Government's contribution to developing and establishing the National Disability Insurance Scheme (NDIS). David commenced working with NDS in 2015 as Victorian State Manager before being appointed Acting CEO at NDS in 2019.

NDS represents service providers across Australia in their work to deliver high-quality supports and life opportunities for people with disability. NDS has more than 1050 member non-government organisations which support people with all forms of disability. Its members collectively provide the full range of disability services – from accommodation support, respite and therapy to community access and employment. NDS provides information and networking opportunities to its members and policy advice to State, Territory and Federal governments.

David, there is so much change in the disability sector, if you had to isolate one or two of the biggest challenges facing your members in 2020 what would they be?

There are many important issues but the first challenge I'd single out would be the inability of the sector to recruit people to deliver services under the NDIS in sufficient numbers and with appropriate qualifications to satisfy the needs of people with disability.

We know from NDS's surveys, analysis and reporting and from other data that there is unmet demand for services and supports. Our members in rural and remote areas are telling us that, for them, it's often a question of just finding any person, and then, in many cases, supporting and training that person to understand how to work in the sector.

The hot issue is the need to grow the workforce by around 70,000 FTE to meet demand. This is the net increase required to support the 460,000 participants once the Scheme is fully rolled out, that is by June 2020. It's fair to say the likelihood of meeting this challenge within that timeframe is pretty remote at this stage.

NDS has been raising these issues with governments over the last six years and even before the Scheme started. NDS has run and facilitated a range of projects in an effort to grow the workforce: our Workforce Connectors project in Victoria, our Work Ability project and similar projects in Queensland, the Workforce Impact Collective in the ACT, the National Disability Practitioners initiative, the innovative workforce fund and, most recently, in our advocacy for a national workforce strategy.

The second key challenge is the Royal Commission into Violence, Abuse, Neglect and Exploitation. As it's a challenge for the sector so it is an opportunity in our view. The Royal Commission will be NDS's key strategic priority for the next three years at least, because it will certainly need to be the key strategic priority for our members.

The Royal Commission's brief is very broad. It will inquire into and interrogate not just the provision of disability services by providers but the experience of people with disability wherever they may be living, working and socialising in the community. NDS supports the Royal Commission and its work. We are looking forward to the opportunity to provide our submission and to give evidence should the Commission require us to.

On the back of that, what would be your key message for providers right now?

In regard to the Royal Commission, our key message is that it's important not to be scared but to be prepared. Make sure you are ready to talk frankly, transparently and honestly about what's happened in the past and where things have gone wrong. Say what you've done to address those issues and ensure that they never happen again. It's also important to be able to identify positive outcomes and how we can embed those outcomes achieved with and for people with disability more broadly within the system.

In terms of workforce issues, I think we'd say to providers that, as best you can within the limitations imposed by capped prices and the assumptions underpinning them, seek to become an employer of choice and market yourself as being part of the fastest growing sector in the Australian economy. Ours is a sector which is going to continue to offer some of the richest opportunities for ongoing employment over the next 10 to 20 years, a sector which is unlikely to be the subject of employment downturns as a result of automation or robotisation, for example. The disability sector is one that literally relies upon the good work of human beings to support other human beings, as you would hope would be the case when our goal is to put the client at the centre of everything we do as providers.

As a sector we need to be more open about sharing our stories of the great outcomes that are being achieved and not be held back by any sense of false modesty. I love the stories our members are able to share about what's been achieved when they have been able to work really well, and with the right resources, with people with disability.

I was fortunate enough to be a guest speaker at the graduation of a number of people with disability who'd completed 26 weeks in open employment. They were thrilled to have a job that was meaningful and substantive; in which they felt appropriately supported and celebrated. Everybody in the room was tearing up. Parents were making spontaneous speeches about the difference that this provider and their staff had made, and it was clear to me that everyone knew the value of the work that was being done and what had been achieved. It was a fantastic experience and reinforced for me the importance of the role played by those organsations and their staff supporting people with disability.

How should providers address the issue of attracting future talent into the disability workforce?

This is a very important question. The responsibility for developing the sector, growing the workforce and enhancing the experience of NDIS participants is multifaceted. I don't think this is a responsibility to be borne by disability providers alone.

There continues to be a role, in my view, for all Australian governments to play, not just in terms of the quantity but in terms of the quality of our workforce as well. We need all governments to understand that the NDIS provides support to only about 10% of people with disability in this country. To leave it to the NDIS to grow the workforce would be, in my view, for governments to abdicate their responsibilities to their citizens.

Providers understand the importance of becoming an employer of choice in a competitive labour market, albeit with the challenges of capped prices, low wage assumptions underpinning prices and often difficult and challenging work.

Providers are implementing a range of measures to attract new starters to our sector however our members are telling us it is still difficult to recruit for certain types of work such as behaviour support practitioners, therapists and psychologists.

Albeit in the context of what is still an immature Scheme, it is unacceptable that an NDIS participant with a significant funding package for appropriate supports is unable to spend their package because there aren't the workers available.

NDS is not naively saying that things must change by tomorrow, however there is sufficient data showing the underutilisation of active supports which may indicate that people are presently unable to access the support workers and services they need in all cases.

The NDIA and the Commonwealth government could constructively be involved in developing with the sector models of local decision making which have a greater chance of taking into account regional workforce issues. We are talking about local knowledge heavily informing planning and support co-ordination in a targeted manner.

How are providers addressing the issue of change fatigue and workplace burnout?

Over the last six years many providers have understandably been challenged by what is a completely different system both in terms of the funding model and structural reforms. Some have found it more challenging than others.

There will be a range of reasons why some providers may be facing change fatigue and workplace burnout. For some, the changes they have been compelled to make have been of a significant magnitude.

What we are talking about is asking a provider (who in the past usually relied upon programmatic locked funding to deliver particular services to particular clients who were brought to their door by the funder) to remodel itself at its own expense and provide individualised supports to an individual consumer engaging in what has been described as a quasi or public sector market.

It's a completely different scale of change. Many people have suggested the NDIS is the biggest social policy initiative in Australia's history since Medicare. I disagree only because I think it's bigger – it is not just funding reform; it is wholesale structural reform as well. That scale of change and the challenges it presents is enough to tire anybody out.

NDS's *State of the Disability Sector Report 2018* showed that 13% of providers surveyed had considered going into administration in the previous 12 months; 28% had made a loss and 62% of those surveyed indicated they had difficulty recruiting a workforce to meet service demands.

Those who aren't at the point of burnout are using this period, post-NDIS roll-out for most, as an opportunity to get customer focused, to realise economies of scale using technology, and embracing consumer demand for in community and at-home support.

I think this trend will continue and will see providers increasingly supporting their staff to work remotely as part of a team. We know there are providers who have already embraced the concept of self-managing or self-leading teams, giving the consumer what they need whilst empowering their workforce to do even better work, in cohesive ways.

Increasingly, providers are seizing the opportunity to really celebrate the successes they are achieving and doing this through a vehicle they have never really had to use before the NDIS: marketing. They are combatting change fatigue and boosting staff morale by more actively promoting great outcomes on LinkedIn, Twitter, Facebook, Instagram and mainstream media. This has the benefit of promoting their organisation but also of reminding their staff of the value and meaning of their work.

I'm also hearing of some providers, particularly those offering Supported Independent Living services, who are opening themselves up to feedback from advocates representing people with disability, to test the quality of the services they are offering. This willingness to be open to new ideas and perspectives will also, I believe assist those organisations in combatting change fatigue.

What role does your culture play within NDS? How do you keep your values 'front of mind'? How do you keep your diverse teams 'connected'?

Communication and consistent messaging is key. We know that our team at NDS shares a deep-seated commitment to supporting our members to deliver quality supports for people with disability so they can lead really great lives.

Our culture is important because we are spread so disparately. We are the only peak body that I'm aware of that currently has a physical presence in every state and territory in Australia. I am inspired by the fact that wherever I go in Australia, I can be confident our staff have been there before me, working and supporting our members.

NDS itself has gone through a significant transformational change culturally as you can expect when your former CEO, Dr Ken Baker AM, leaves after 18 years in the job, which is an unusually long time for a CEO, particularly one as well respected as Ken was when he left.

As a team we have identified the values we want to bring to our work. We talk about respect, leadership, innovation, collaboration and teamwork, accountability and integrity. Where I want to get to is that, rather than being a poster on a wall, they define what it means to work at NDS.

I'm a great believer in the phrase, *'that which we walk past becomes the standard'*. We need to do more than merely talk about the values; it's about how we live them. That starts from the top and works its way across the organisation.

Increasingly we'll be a non-hierarchical organisation; one which recognises what people bring to the table wherever they may be in their role and leverages their talents. Ours is a sector which lives and breathes on the energy of people and so it is for NDS as a peak body.

We're becoming an organisation which is less office based and more 'out and about' – a people and place model – with our staff working where our members are or using technology to ensure our members don't have to come to us. I'm not saying that technology delivers culture but it does support culture where it supports better communication and engagement.

Our Workforce Connectors program is an example of where being regionally based in Victoria is a positive virtue. I rarely see members of that team in the office because they are out working with our members in the regions where they live and work. So it was in the case of our staff in QLD, working in the WorkAbility project.

We encourage our staff to be proud of where they work and to become more prominently involved in social media. We have very active Twitter accounts and LinkedIn pages and a new Facebook site. So we're using social media to not only promote NDS but also implicitly and explicitly to remind our staff of the work that is being done. Yammer has become a valuable internal communications tool. I make a point of posting on it as regularly as I can to keep our staff updated on where I am, what I'm doing and celebrating what I'm seeing in our work.

For many providers, the focus on audits and compliance is swamping the focus on the participant experience. How can providers support their teams without compromising the actual customer experience?

I'd start from first principles by saying that registered providers who, by definition, are complying with the Quality and Safeguards Framework, have a really strong story to tell their current and future clients: That they are committed to working to a high level of quality in the services and supports they provide.

NDS has, for some time, supported a nationally consistent quality and safeguarding framework underpinned by legislation for the whole of Australia. We don't think that self-regulation is appropriate because regulation done well actually grows positive outcomes in the sector. It also helps ensure that those who are not meeting appropriate standards are less likely to remain part of our sector.

We are in the very early stages of the Quality and Safeguards Framework. It's fair to say that because of this, many members are experiencing significant issues working within it and understanding it.

Depending on which state or territory you're in, you are at a different point in the change continuum in moving to the national framework. There are some states where formal regulation was less in evidence than in others. Providers in those states (through no fault of their own) have a greater distance to travel to meet the expectations set by the Framework.

As Acting CEO, what role do you play in driving the culture at NDS and how does this work on a practical daily basis?

I see my role as being to support the development of a culture in which good ideas, insights and initiatives could come from any-where in the organisation. We need to have in place feedback loops which allow this to happen. We have just recently dipped our organisational toe into the concept of Lean Thinking. It's still very early days, but I think it's a way of working we can adopt to identify those processes and administration which are clunky. We used to be a federated organisation and we are now a national peak body and that change process has a tendency to create duplication which we need to sweep away to be come as effective and efficient for our members as possible.

How does NDS measure its staff and member experience?

We surveyed our staff at the end of last year and received really interesting feedback. It's given me a lot to think about in terms of what an action plan to address the issues raised should look like. With such a disparate workforce, our staff need to be better sup-ported by management in terms of being recognised for their skills and abilities. There is work that we can be doing through a number of mechanisms I referred to earlier.

In regard to our member experience, we recently completed our annual Members' Survey which returned a positive response from members that almost 75% were positive or very positive about their experience with NDS. But I'd be lying if I said that every member was positive about their NDS membership. Indeed I've got a ream of paper from members about where they think we could improve. Thankfully, I think you learn more from the negatives than you do from the positives so there's plenty for us to think about!

I'm under no illusions that in this period of post-NDIS rollout, our members are looking to NDS to be strong in our advocacy on issues that matter to them; to be developing and delivering programs and services to support their organisations to deliver great services that people with disability value; and to do better at communicating using a wider range of technology and social media than we have done in the past.

Our virtual conference model has been an absolute winner with our members so far. Our quality and safeguarding virtual conference, which ran for a day, featured a series of webinars which attracted more than 1200 registrants. We have members working in the community and in remote and very remote parts of Australia, so the prospect of them getting to a capital city let alone to a conference centre is precisely zip.

In early September, we did a live web stream for more than 240 members on the Royal Commission. I see this sort of technology as a way of ensuring we are able engage with our members directly albeit that we may not always be within handshake distance.

It's great when NDS can do those sorts of things, which take account of where our members are working and that their priority is always to provide quality disability services.

Ours is a sector which increasingly has to be thinking in terms of running disability service organisations as businesses. As businesses which are purpose driven but which are businesses nevertheless.

Our members know that those who are going to thrive under the NDIS in the future will be those that understand forensically the importance of having the commercial acumen and business sense to iterate, innovate and deliver for the people they are working for: people with disability.

Chapter 5 ▶

Step 2: Build Your Internal Brand

'Your brand is a promise. And it all starts with the people who will keep that promise.'

Allanna Kelsall, Chief People Officer, RSL Queensland

In March 2018 I was invited to speak at an interstate conference for disability service providers. During my presentation I showed a slide with some pictures of billboards, brochures, Facebook pages, video thumbnails and banners – all containing the same sort of imagery and exactly the same messaging.

The problem, I explained, was that these pictures were taken from the marketing materials of 10 or more different disability service providers in NSW and Victoria. There was no differentiation.

Following the launch of the NDIS in these states, many organisations launched expensive mainstream marketing campaigns with homogenous content. Their competitors had become their benchmark, not their customers. The result? Just a lot of noise, wasted marketing budgets, and an increasingly confused, anxious customer.

The point I wanted them to understand that day was that it's very easy to waste a lot of money with undifferentiated mainstream marketing tactics, particularly when disability service provision is actually a local business and your customer is simply looking for a local provider they can trust.

Jill spends $100k

That evening at the 'conference drinks and networking' session, I was approached by a CEO (let's call her Jill) saying she had just signed off on a $100,000 marketing strategy and she would like me to review it as soon as possible. I agreed without any thought to asking for payment; after all, she'd just handed me a glass of champagne.[21]

Following a flurry of emails over the next few days, I found time to review her 'strategy'. The news wasn't good. Jill had just approved a campaign that consisted only of TV advertising and a website build. This was *not* actually a marketing strategy. It was a scattershot awareness campaign. There was no clear value proposition or call to action, no clear customer profile or segment; there was no indication as to how they would measure success; there was no indication of any prior consumer research to justify the creative content. This was advertising on steroids dressed up as a marketing strategy (although my response to Jill was more diplomatic than that).

Marketing redefined

Before I can begin to discuss why marketing and branding are relevant to organisational culture, I'd like to revisit some fundamental definitions. Because how you define marketing and branding will make all the difference to your ability to successfully use the cultural change framework outlined in this book.

Most people (like Jill) define marketing in terms of tactics: websites, brochures, logos, Facebook, SEO, point of sale, TV, events, social media and videos. But this stuff is only the tip of the iceberg.

---

21   This is something my accountant keeps raising with me.

For any of it to work (that is, make a positive, measurable difference to your business) it has to be underpinned by a genuine understanding of your customers' needs and how you might be uniquely positioned to serve those needs and earn their trust.

If you are faced with a highly competitive market and a limited marketing budget you simply cannot afford to spend precious funds without a solid strategy.

A successful market-driven strategy requires getting crystal clear on two things:

- **Who is your customer?** What are their specific unmet needs? You must understand how those needs are changing, what their burning frustrations are, their preferred communication channels and who they already trust.

- **What need do you serve?** This is a lot bigger than it sounds. It means you need to be crystal clear on who you are and who you aren't. You need to be clear on why you exist, the values you stand for, the change you are seeking, and the services you excel in. From all these things will flow your unique value proposition, the stories you share and the key messages that different groups of people will actually sit up and listen to.

If you don't have a customer, you don't have a business. There are two definitions of marketing that really bring this point home. The first is from Peter Drucker:

> **Marketing is so basic that it cannot be considered a separate function. It is the whole business seen from the point of view of its final result, that is, from the customer's point of view.**

The second definition is from Seth Godin's wonderful book *This is Marketing*:

> **Marketing is the generous act of helping someone solve a problem. Their problem. It's a chance to change the culture for the better. Marketing involves very little in the way of shouting, hustling or coercion. It's a chance to serve, instead.**

If you are willing to accept either of these definitions then your marketing will suddenly become so much more cost effective. Suddenly every contact (and every missed contact) with every customer sends a message of some kind. How you answer the phone, how you dress, how punctual you are – every interaction sends a message about what you value, about what matters to you. Every contact contributes to the customer's 360-degree experience of your organisation and tells them about your brand and what it actually stands for.

Because marketing is a whole-of-organisation function, every single person in your organisation is a living, breathing brand ambassador.

Branding redefined

A brand is so much more than a logo on a page or a screen or a coffee cup. A brand acts as the emotional, human 'glue' between an individual and an organisational entity. It gives that entity a human personality and human characteristics.

Human beings are social beings. We prefer to belong to a tribe who values what we value. When people are loyal to a brand they are loyal because that brand represents something *they* value or something they want others to see in *them* by association. They *trust* that values association.

It's why some people queue outside Apple stores. It's why some people only wear Nike.

I used to define a brand as: 'A declaration of who you are and what you stand for.' But then I realised that I'd missed something really important. Identity is only held in the eye of the beholder, as a result: *you don't own your brand – your customer does.*

A better definition is from Jeff Bezos, Founder & CEO of Amazon:

**Branding is what people say about you
when you're not in the room.**

You can say whatever you like about how great your organisation is and what it stands for and the work you do, but it means nothing if it doesn't match your customers' actual experience. Like marketing, branding is a whole-of-organisation function.

Getting your brand seen, heard and felt

According to the *Huffington Post* (2018), the average internet surfer is served a staggering 11,250 advertisements a day. This 'noise' makes it much harder for marketers to actually connect with customers.

To do this, we need to make our brands personal. We need to reflect a consistent brand personality which earns the trust of our customer. This is particularly true for the stressed customer or decision maker because stressed customers rely on trusted experts.

The internal brand

In my previous book I outlined the three key functions of the non-profit brand as:

1. To build awareness and trust in external audiences. (The external brand.)

2. To build internal cohesion by creating team alignment between the individual's personal values and the organisation's values. (The internal brand.)

3. To drive fundraising, advocacy and the long-term social impacts of your Mission.

It's the second function that's often referred to as the 'internal brand', and it's how strong brands build trust.

Every strong brand is underpinned by strong values that are actually 'lived' on a daily basis by every employee. Every action, every activity and every performance review is framed around these values.

When an employee feels that their personal values are strongly aligned with those of the organisation they work for, you can begin to deliver an unbeatable customer experience, provided the organisational culture is actually living those values. The internal brand *is* your cultural anchor.

Living 'safety'

Years ago, everything at Qantas had to reflect their one brand value. From the height of the flight attendants' heels to the design of the cockpit. That value was *safety*. It was adopted from DuPont, the company who held the OH&S contract with Qantas. This French organisation was founded in 1802 by Éleuthère Irénée du Pont, the man who discovered gunpowder. The story goes that whenever there was a gunpowder test, there would always be a member of du Pont's own family at the site, to demonstrate to his employees that he valued their safety as much as that of his own family.

Your brand purpose

In his book *Start with Why*, Simon Sinek says, 'People don't buy what you do; they buy *why* you do it.' In commercial language, your 'brand purpose' is why your brand exists, your Mission.

Apple's *why* is to 'think differently'. Coco-Cola's brand purpose is 'happiness'. For Bangarra Dance Theatre, the Australian Indigenous dance company, their mission (or brand purpose) is to create 'inspiring experiences that change society'.

For non-profit organisations, the 'brand purpose' is their Mission statement. Once you start thinking like this, the brand becomes one with the Mission and it applies across the entire organisation, not just the marketing function.

If you are seeking a competitive edge in a crowded market then a strong brand purpose becomes the starting point for every leadership decision. Does our marketing support the brand? Does our structure support the brand? Do our employees reflect the brand?

Linking your internal and external brand

In any organisation with a strong, high-performance culture you will find an alignment around the fundamentals (vision, mission, values) which builds trust and cohesion. That alignment also links the internal brand (your brand as experienced by your employees) to the external brand (as experienced by the public).

Your brand and the values it stands for must be understood by every single person in your organisation.

The internal brand is concerned with your internal messaging and communications. In times of change, you need to over-communicate with your employees, keeping people in the loop on the transition: your strategies, what you know and what you don't know yet, the structural changes ahead, what it means for them, what it means for you, where your priorities lie, how you will communicate with them going forward. How frequently you communicate with them goes directly to building trust.

Your team needs to hear from the CEO firsthand what is expected of them and their managers. You need to link the organisation's values to their daily behaviours. They need to feel that the organisation is remaining true to its founding purpose.

The external brand is also built on *trust* (not billboards, websites or brochures). Your customer experience is a direct result of your employee experience. When your culture reinforces your brand values, your employees are supported to live those values and your customers' experience will begin to consistently exceed their expectations.

Creating a great culture requires that every employee is supported to actually live the values or 'bring the brand alive'. For example, if you say you stand for *respect* – how neatly do you dress? How punctual are you? Do you provide new staff with sufficient training to do their job well? Do you look up when they come to your door?

We'll get into this in more detail in chapter 7.

Linking your internal and external brand

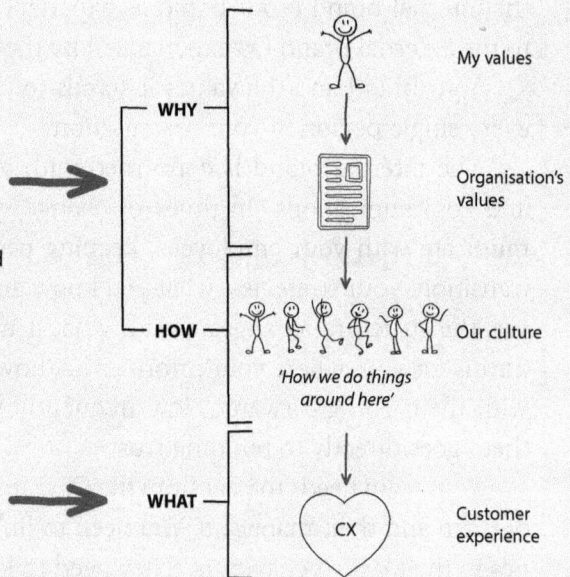

Internal marketing builds employee engagement. It links your brand values to daily behaviours to create the actual customer experience.

The internal brand is built on TRUST
It drives your culture by linking employees to the organisation and your values to daily behaviours. Your employees feel a shared identity, mission and direction.

The external brand is also built on TRUST
When your workplace culture lives your values, the result is a consistently superior customer experience.

WHY — My values

Organisation's values

HOW — Our culture
'How we do things around here'

WHAT — CX Customer experience

Storytelling: the heart of culture

Values and stories build culture, not HR processes and systems. Values are the reason that someone will or won't feel they 'belong' to a community. Stories are how you share those values. Your stories demonstrate that perhaps here is someone who can be trusted.

Storytelling lies at the heart of culture. Your stories are the human element that people sit up and listen to. They help people engage with your mission. Nothing beats an authentic story told with passion.

Stories connect people on an entirely new level, and in so doing they remind us of our shared humanity. They don't need to be polished; they just need to be authentic, well-structured and, if possible, told in the first person.

The Invisible Australians

Below is an excerpt from a presentation I gave to a group of professional men and women who had no lived experience of people with intellectual disability. The response I received from the audience that day reminded me of the simple power of authentic storytelling.

Before we can begin to create a more inclusive, kinder Australia we need to begin to *see the person*, not the disability. The problem is that so often we simply don't see people with disabilities as people with individual longings, dreams and rights. The right to meaningful work, the right to have friends who aren't simply paid to be their friends, the right to live how they choose and with whom they choose, the right to be seen, heard and valued. We only *see* their disability.

Imagine the loneliness you would feel if you discovered that your 'friends', the people you hung out with every day, were actually paid to hang out with you? How would you feel if this happened to your child?

Many years ago I was working as a fundraising consultant for a small disability service provider in Sydney. The role involved me being in their offices three days a week. One of the many rewarding joys of my day was the welcome note I would find on my desk each morning from a young lady named Valerie who attended their 'supported employment' services.

Valerie was a warm, vivacious teenager who loved sailing and singing. I will never forget her 17th birthday. We'd organised a small surprise birthday party for Valerie just before the end of the day. All the clients and staff squeezed into the small kitchen and gathered around a table to sing *Happy Birthday* as she noisily blew out the candles on her birthday cake.

Then I noticed a man standing at the back of the kitchen whom I hadn't seen before. A tall, skinny guy about my age – with tears rolling down his face.

It was Valerie's Dad.

He shared with me that he was just so grateful that somebody else had bought a cake and sung Happy Birthday to his beautiful girl. He went on to tell me that he was raising three kids on his own and that this hadn't happened before. It was the first time that somebody else had bought her a cake.

It was the smallest thing. But that birthday cake meant the world to Valerie's dad.

We need to see people with disabilities as people, not as a label. If you pass someone with any kind of disability on the street, if you're standing next to them in a shop or sitting next to someone on the bus – don't look the other way or pretend they aren't there. Make an effort, reach out and say hi.

And teach your kids to do the same. So that this 'invisibility' ends with this generation.

So that if one day your granddaughter or grandson is born with a disability, then they might have the opportunity to be seen for the individuals they are, they will have genuine friends, they will have choices and they will be valued.

When I finished speaking the room went silent. I shared Valerie's story that day because I knew that most of the people in that room were parents, and I wanted a story that would resonate with them. I will never forget how every single person came up to me afterwards to share the impact of that simple story.

Stories connect people

The act of authentic storytelling connects hearts and minds. If you read this entire book and only take away this fact then you've still learned a lot.

As a kid I was a weekly boarder at a school on the other side of Sydney. Far enough away so that it wasn't easy for me to sneak out and get home. I'll never forget coming home on a Friday afternoon and the joy it was to see the kitchen table covered in my favourite food; Sara Lee apple 'pull-aparts', ham sandwiches, donuts … you name it. (I'd usually buy a chicken-and-lettuce toasted sandwich at Town Hall station on the way home and just make sure I'd eaten it before I'd walked in the door.)

My mum would want to hear all about my week. She'd sit down and listen for hours to what had happened; she'd want to hear all my stories and she would share hers. I just remember the laughing and the eating. Dad would walk in about 7 pm, shocked to see that we were still enjoying afternoon tea.

This was the gift my mum gave me: her time. She was an extremely patient, kind, generous woman who always had time to hear my stories.

How 10,000 camels created one team

One of the best icebreakers I have ever used in a workshop is one I came up with two years ago while working for an organisation with multiple internal silos. I now use it at the start of every workshop because it changes the energy in the room.

It's this: *share one thing that nobody in the room knows about you.* It changes the dynamic energy of the room because we consciously have to make the shift from sharing information to sharing stories. Facts simply aren't as powerful as stories when it comes to compelling listening material.

In a recent Culture Masterclass I faced 24 people from eight different organisations. I was concerned whether the group would be able to work as a team. If they couldn't then they wouldn't get the outcomes I'd promised from the workshop. Things were initially quiet – until the icebreaker. One lady shared her narrow escape from a civil war in Rwanda; another had recently been on a 'brothel tour' of Kalgoorlie. Another played the tenor horn; another was an equestrian.

However, the turning point for the workshop was when a CEO in the room shared his 'one thing'. He told a story about visiting the Holy Land with his family. During that trip he was offered 10,000 camels in exchange for his wife. Suddenly, the room cracked up and everyone wanted to know more. *Did he negotiate? That's a lot of camels? Did he take the deal? Is she very attractive?*

From that moment on, I was working with 24 people who shared and worked as if they were one team. It was unbelievable the level of honest communication that day.

How stories 'ground' meetings

A great way to 'ground' a team meeting and keep your values top of mind is to start it by asking for mobiles off and laptops off. This immediately shifts things. Then ask that every person shares one thing from the last week that reflects one of the organisation's values in action. This simple initiative does a few things to reinforce a positive culture:

- It ensures that people's brains are in the room not on their last activity. It gets people present and listening, not staring at their devices.

- Your team starts to look for stories to take to your weekly meeting. You begin to develop a culture of storytelling.

- Your employees begin to see that we don't just talk about our values, we live them.

- The meeting begins with a focus on what really matters. The 'important' is not hijacked by the 'urgent'.

Story types you can use in your organisation

Annette Simmons in her excellent book *Whoever Tells The Best Story Wins* makes the point that we need to pay better attention to the stories we are already telling every day, and the impact they have on our lives and the lives of others. How many of us use face-to-face opportunities to share how stressed we are, or our war stories? A lot of people do this. But venting our frustrations doesn't help with people we wish to influence. Everybody needs to vent at times, but your managers need to be aware of when it's appropriate and when it's cultural arson. Remember, culture is a top-down process.

There are so many different types of stories you can tell to spread your brand and engage, influence and inspire your team, your clients, your donors and your partners. As a self-taught fundraiser I learnt very early on that we human beings are hard-wired to sit up and listen to stories about individuals. But tell a story about hundreds or thousands of people and your listeners switch off. It makes no sense, but it's true. So, to maximise the impact of your story, you need to keep it about an individual.

It might be helpful to break down the types of stories that can build your culture …

Your organisation's origin story

We've already touched on this biggie. It's the single most important story for building a strong culture for three reasons:

- It demonstrates *why* your organisation came into being – the need your founders identified that had to be addressed.

- It connects the organisation with its mission or purpose; it connects the past with the present and today with your future.

- It demonstrates that you are continuing to fulfil your original mission with new relevance in the local communities you serve.

The origin story is, in effect, your mission story. In the absence of this shared story, employees lose a sense of meaning and direction and cultures fragment.

As Laura O'Reilly, CEO of Fighting Chance, mentioned to me in her interview for this book:

> **The origin story *is* our culture. Storytelling – and the origin story in particular – is the most important tool in our armoury. We also empower others to tell their origin story. For example, why did *they* say 'yes' to working with Fighting Chance? Why are they here?**

The CEO's story

Who are you as a person? Tell us about your family, your first job. Make it personal. Your employees and customers need to know why they should trust you.

The CEO's story is basically a 'who I am' story that moves into a 'why I'm here' story. It's a natural segue into why she or he is personally committed to the organisation's mission. You'll often see interviews with business leaders who successfully use their personal story as a vehicle for sharing the values that drive their organisation. Think Richard Branson (Virgin), Phil Knight (Nike), Australian CEO

Tom Daunt of Aldi or Vittoria Coffee's Les Schirato.[22] You don't have to be an extrovert; you just have to know how to tell your story.

The individual 'values-in-action' stories

This could be an employee story, a client story, a donor story, a family member or carer story. Make it authentic, make it personal and use great imagery. Today it is easier than ever to record a video on your phone and upload it to YouTube or LinkedIn. Often the lower the production values, the greater your credibility. You need to look real, not polished. Genuine, not slick.

Video can make compulsive viewing. Instagram stories and Snapchat are other great ways to get a story out there. Pick the best channel based on who you're targeting. The great thing is that any digital native (that is, most people aged 35 and under) can usually pull a great video together for a tiny fraction of an outside agency.

Some final tips: if you do outsource the work to an external agency, don't let them tell you what your customer should say or how they should be portrayed. Let your existing customers tell you. Insist on clear, measurable outcomes from every marketing spend.[23]

Some essential elements for great storytelling

Some essential elements for great storytelling are:

- Be authentic. (The less 'slick', the greater the credibility.)

- Tell it in the first person if possible; share something of yourself.

- Add visuals if possible. (According to behavioural research compiled by 3M, the company behind Post It Notes, our brains process images 60,000 times faster than text.)

---

22   Case studies are included in 'The Workplace Culture & the NDIS Workbook', available for download from www.fcmarketing.com.au.

23   You will find a simple story structure template in the abovementioned workbook.

- Keep it simple and structure your story. Your narrative has to follow clear and specific steps.

- Target the content to your audience. They must be able to relate to it.

- Keep videos at 30 to 60 seconds; think in 'story bites'.

Summary

▶ How you define marketing and branding makes all the difference.

▶ Strong brands are underpinned by values that make them personal.

▶ The internal brand acts as a cultural anchor.

▶ The brand purpose must be your Mission.

▶ A strong culture requires internal and external brand alignment.

▶ Stories beat other forms of communication hands down. Storytelling lies at the heart of culture because stories connect hearts and minds.

▶ We need to be aware of the stories we are already sharing.

▶ Cultures are built on the origin story, the CEO's story and the individual values-in-action stories.

▶ We need to know, share and practise the essential elements of great storytelling.

Interview

Melinda Kubisa, CEO, Community Living Options, SA

Melinda Kubisa had been with Community Living Options (CLO) for 17 years prior to her appointment as CEO in 2017. CLO was established in Victor Harbor in 1982 by a group of local parents who wanted respite and accommodation for their adult children. They didn't want their children to be forced to move far away, or into an institution. They wanted their children to have the opportunity to thrive and live in their local community, and Community Living Options was born. Since 1982 CLO has seen outstanding growth. Today, CLO is financially robust. Their 550 staff provide services in Adelaide, South Adelaide, Victor Harbour and Kangaroo Island. CLO's unique service strength lies in its evidence-based model of positive and therapeutic supports for people with complex high level forensic disability and dual disability. Over the last 10 years, considerable growth has come from supporting people who are in and out of the prison and hospital systems.

What role does your culture play at CLO? How does your brand support that culture? How do you keep your values top of mind?

To me culture is critical, it's pivotal. When I think about how our brand supports that culture, I've come up with the fact that the brand has to *be* your culture.

In the *Bringing the Brand Alive Program* you ran for us, we talked about people finding our culture fast paced, very action orientated and we came up with the term 'high velocity'. We all have values, but what separates you? Our culture is our differentiator. It's why we're successful and it is what builds our brand and reputation.

Last week I was speaking at the ASID (Australasian Society for Intellectual Disability) conference about knowing your model and entrenching that framework within your values. We have a human-rights-based, person-centred model that is entrenched within our values. If everyone is living and breathing our model *that* is our culture and that becomes our brand.

Culture is now more important than it ever was before, because we are entering the NDIS. The brand must now deliver excellence in a consumer market and culture is critical in creating a focused strategy that flows throughout the organisation.

In the first year of our marketing plan we focused on style guides, logos, advertising and all of those things that were about getting visibility in a new market. To launch the second year of our marketing plan we engaged your program. This helped us understand how we could use our values and culture to bring the brand alive on a daily basis. The process also really helped us identify and focus on our UVP (unique value proposition) and identify which stories to tell to which audiences. I can give you examples of the stories I've told and the different successes we've had since then. It has been a fabulous mechanism from bottom up/top down to define who we are and to help everyone feel part of one whole.

Through that program, the collaboration between marketing and leadership was born at CLO. So, to me now, culture at CLO is driven by that whole-of-organisation collaboration between marketing and leadership. The two are so entwined now, since your program that our next level of transformation is through a whole organisation approach.

Things are falling into place. People are showing up differently. To answer the last bit of your question, how do we keep our values top of mind ... I feel like we continue to articulate and embed these values at the core of everything we do. If your values remain strong and are constantly embedded, then you're going to be more flexible to the environment around you. It means that whatever comes up – we will be able to respond to it. We have a criteria for finding the optimal response, regardless of the situation.

Does your organisational structure support your culture? How has it changed in response to the NDIS?

Again, through the strategic planning process *and* your program this year, I now feel that structure and culture have a very causal relationship. That's the best way to put it.

Structure is the key to both culture and organisational performance. A lot of people talk about developing a strategy supporting structure, but it has to be culture *and* strategy supporting structure. Culture is integral to driving the strategy forward and delivering the outcomes. To respond to the NDIS you have to decentralise the structures. It goes without saying that you have to really expect your frontline workers and co-ordinators to make decisions and *be* the centre for the family.

Leadership is critical. If you want to have staff as a differentiator you need to invest in leadership. Both your structure and your culture need to reflect the values held by the organisation. But it is the leadership behaviours that drive outcomes.

Looking at how our structure changed in response to the NDIS; there has been so much change! It's all about having the right person in the right job. Some of the changes include:

- A new Service Development Co-ordinator position, which is a customer on-boarding role. I also invested in frontline management and moved from 5 to 13 frontline co-ordinators to invest in staff supervision, monitoring and support.

- I have added an entire clinical team that work with a Clinical Services Manager.

- A new Senior Manager Operations with business skills, leadership skills and commercial acumen.

- I also implemented a new quality position, delivering excellence and actually assessing quality across the organisation.

- Our marketing co-ordinator position is now a business development manager role.

- We invested in our HR department by looking at a dedicated training and development role. We now have a whole resource dedicated to frontline manager training.

- We also prepared a governance skills matrix and looked at the skillset of our board and have done much board recruiting this year to build a values-based board that is both market driven and mission driven with various business skills and expertise.

As CEO, what role do you feel you play in creating the culture and communicating the vision at CLO?

The role of CEO is critical; it needs to drive the culture and communicate the vision. It has to come from the top down; they need to see me leading by example. I think the culture and the vision is the *collective soul of an organisation*. I don't know if that term has been coined before but if I actually don't drive that collective soul, people don't have that vehicle for motivating, empowering and inspiring others to achieve that vision.

I also believe that you have to have clarity around your expectations. You need to be on the bus. So I need to articulate that vision and culture at every point, so people are either on this bus or they decide to get off the bus and go somewhere else. So that is around engaging, supporting and coaching employees. But it's also about strong performance management. The two have to go together to achieve that vision.

So, I do believe I am pivotal in setting the frameworks, the models, the strategies that deliver on the vision. We like a lot of data; some would call us data centric. So I get my team to measure three things: their social impact, their customer satisfaction and their employee satisfaction. They do this through consumer questionnaires, surveys and satisfaction ratings and employee culture surveys, pulse checks.

In creating that positive culture here, as CEO, I need to show people that I am hungry for feedback and continuous improvement. I like to constantly ask about what isn't working and why people think it isn't working and what we can learn from experiences.

How important is your origin story to your culture?

My answer to this is actually quite simple. *Our origin story is pivotal. It's the centre of our culture. It's why we exist. This is where our culture begins. It is family centred, person centred. I never want to lose this story! It is our foundation. It's becoming a key attraction for staff; it's the first thing people mention in their interviews. So, for me* **it is what makes it real.**

How do you attract the talent you need and ensure your team members are a values fit?

Over the last year we have been rolling out values-based, person-centred recruitment, a new methodology. We don't have the data yet to say that it has particularly increased our retention, but we are still attracting talent in a tight marketplace. When benchmarked to the sector, we are remaining strong and able to attract and retain our talent.

The culture shift is that we expect the values first and we will teach you the skills, or support you to get the competencies. From leadership through to the frontline, if people are a values fit they stay longer and we have better outcomes.

Are you looking to recruit from outside the sector as well?

Values-based recruitment is the key. We look outside the disability sector for our leadership and business development positions. We keep reviewing our induction processes. After your program, we developed a strong three-day induction program followed by a very structured 12-week orientation.

What do you think are the biggest challenges facing the disability sector right now? If you had one key message for other CEOs/other providers what would it be?

I think the biggest challenge is workforce capacity and capability. The prime demand is for quality workers. Retaining talent has to be a focus in addressing that challenge.

Financial sustainability is still a challenge for many CEOs.

I also believe that being able to set yourself apart in a competitive market, understanding your UVP, how to distinguish yourself and how to do that in a crowded market is really challenging for disability providers. It's not something they are used to.

If you can identify that niche then sustainability becomes so much easier.

Know what you do well and do it. Stay true to that core. Don't be everything. Know your capabilities; know your limitations. Under the NDIS, you've got to be so flexible, adaptable, responsive and ready for change. So that's why I say: know what you do, do it well, invest in your people and your leadership, then you will be ready.

Our niche is complex disability, including mental health. We stayed very clear on that. It is our core capability and we do it very well. We were poised for an opportunity when pyscho-social disability rolled out, so we stayed strong and were poised to capitalise on that opportunity when it emerged.

Interview

Anita Bayford, Chief Operations Officer, disAbility Living Inc.

disAbility Living was established over 30 years ago by a group of families to provide person-centred services for their children entering adulthood. Today, they provide services to people in the community who live with acquired brain injury, physical and neurological disorders, intellectual disability, autism and mental health conditions. They offer a range of services including therapy, mentoring, community participation, in-home support and short-term accommodation for both children and adults, as well as long-term supported independent living options for adults. Their culture is strongly supported by a rigorous values matrix called 'CREDIT' and a dynamic, customer focused organisational structure.

Anita, what role does your culture play at disAbility Living Inc.? How important is it? How do you keep your values 'front of mind' for your teams?

Our culture drives decision making at all levels from our board of directors to everyday service delivery. It's at the front, in the middle, and behind everything we say and do. It's an important part of who we are as individuals, and as an organisation; a shared awareness, alignment and understanding between us that plays an important role in uniting us.

Our organisational core values are inherent in the character of all our employees. We present these values through our 'CREDIT' culture, designed by our CEO and a team of staff some 8 to 10 years ago, and thriving. CREDIT is an acronym for:

- Communication

- Respect

- Empowerment

- Dignity

- Insight

- Trust

We keep our values (or 'CREDIT') front of mind by building the terminology into everyday conversations and constantly referring to CREDIT in our decision making.

Person-centred tools are also used to drive our culture. These include but aren't limited to templates such as 'one-page profiles' that we encourage all clients and staff to have, as well as 'working/ not working' and '4 plus 1' conversation templates. We also form meetings around 'the positive meeting guidelines' of Helen Sanderson and Mary Beth Lepkowsy.[24]

We recently participated in your Culture Masterclass and what we have taken away from that day is the 'Bringing the Brand Alive' tool which will help us to develop new workflows and identify those touchpoints where there are traffic jams, anomalies or confusion for our employees.

Our CREDIT culture is also reinforced through our training programs. We provide employees with comprehensive training in CREDIT. The content of this training is adapted as we evolve, our current review emphasising outstanding customer service.

We follow initial training with a session we call 'A Day in the Life'. This is a fun day engaging in activities that underpin our culture by actually experiencing what it might be like to be on the receiving end of our services (for example, using a wheelchair, communicating with adaptive equipment, receiving support with meals and personal care such as teeth cleaning).

Essentially we use every opportunity we can to reinforce our values, both formally and informally through day-to-day

---

24 Helen Sanderson and Mary Beth Lepkowsky, *Person Centred Teams: A practical guide to delivering personalisation through effective team work.*

communication, social media, meetings, forums, training and special events such as family fun days and other celebrations.

How have you changed your organisational structure to better support your culture (especially frontline staff) and the customer experience under the NDIS?

We originated from a very small family-based organisation set up by families to ensure their loved ones receive quality whole-of-life support. We value this history and the qualities of a family-friendly approach, acknowledging that everyone can offer valuable insight supporting clients to articulate their needs and wants and identifying what is required to make it happen.

We've turned our structure upside down, positioning clients and direct support workers central to everything. We select our staff using CREDIT, nurture them, support them and train them to provide the best possible service.

It's also important to note the informal relationships that occur throughout disAbility Living. Culturally our organisation is quite unique in dispensing with hierarchy and formalities when it comes to how we engage with each other. We value the input of everyone, and it isn't unusual for our CEO to communicate directly with our frontline workers. We don't let titles and roles get in the way of relationships that enrich lives and foster positive outcomes. It's very important for everyone to feel valued and part of the organisation.[25]

Our Staff Engagement Team have the privilege of overseeing our staff ensuring they are fully supported throughout their career with us. We're consistently looking at how we structure our teams and roles to create better pathways for professional development and career progression.

My own role as Chief Operations Officer oversees the operational component of the organisation with other departments set up

---

25 A copy of disAbility Living's organisational chart can be found in 'The Workplace Culture & the NDIS Workbook', available for download from www.fcmarketing.com.au.

to provide support to the operational team. This is a big change from past structures and roles.

For example, the Finance team have historically been the people to 'set the budget' for each department using block-funded income. With the introduction of NDIS, and a person-centred approach, our contracts are directly with our clients, with budgets set to ensure that service provision is strictly according to individual participant plans, schedules of services and service agreements, with administrative costs dispersed across other departments who are held accountable to work within their budgets.

How have you changed your induction and performance management to reflect your values and support your culture?

We ensure a corporate induction is facilitated by all senior staff. This provides all staff an opportunity to meet, get to know and feel comfortable in approaching senior staff. It's also a great opportunity for senior staff to share the 'real them' including 'fun facts' about themselves. This humanises each manager as opposed to being known by their workplace role alone.

Staff are then provided appropriate orientation and induction within their department or work site which is led by their supervisor.

Office-based staff, managers and team leaders are also provided with a comprehensive 'meet and greet' program, spending time with each of the departmental managers to learn what the department can do to assist their role. This orientation breaks down 'us and them' barriers and increases understanding of 'who to go to for what'. Most importantly, it builds common threads as human beings in terms of learning about each other, including personal interests, commonalities and so on.

With regard to performance management, we refocused our HR team, the 'Staff Engagement Team', to 'be there' for the employee to fully support a person-centred approach. The supervising manager will address the problem from an organisational perspective with a staff engagement team's role being to support the staff member.

We strongly encourage *all* staff to engage in 'reflection meetings' with their supervisor at least once every three months. Annual appraisals occur, but for our team leaders and all managers we also have a professional performance 360° review process.

How do you go about attracting future talent?

Like all service providers currently operating in the disability sector, we're confronted with sourcing skilled and experienced staff with predictions of twice the number of staff required to meet demand across Australia over the next few years. This year alone we have increased our staff pool by 65%.

Our culture is certainly something that attracts staff. Our name and our reputation do rate well when potential staff are questioned on why they want to work for us. Word-of-mouth sharing of information by staff and clients can never be underestimated, as it is our primary source for new clients and many staff joining the team. In recent months we have observed staff choosing to transfer their employment to disAbility Living when the client they support changes their service providers to disAbility Living.

We have incentives for staff to refer potential recruits. However, we are selective about who we employ, which can cause delays recruiting in a timely manner as we never stray from prioritising a good 'fit' with our culture.

Of course, we use social media and career websites to promote roles, but a lot of our appointments are through internal promotion. It's important to know what a Community Support Worker (CSW) has done in their past life/roles as their career can take an interesting change of direction if they so choose.

For example, we had a CSW working hands-on with clients while studying accounting – he had a conversation at one of his reflection meetings with his team leader that led to some volunteer work within our finance department to assist with his studies. A year on and he is employed solely in our finance team doing the job he really wants to do.

Our emerging team leader program had six high performers working to develop their skills in readiness for team leader roles – five of the six have been successfully appointed to higher duty roles.

We invest time in supporting the development of a reasonably high volume of student placements. We have a good appointment rate based on their performance and fit for the organisation.

How do you measure employee satisfaction at disAbility Living Inc? What are the key employee data points that providers should be collecting in order to really understand the customer experience?

Employee satisfaction can be difficult to measure because at any one time employees can have a different opinion.

NDIS has been an amazing journey as organisations work hard to educate themselves, their staff and their clients. Some staff welcome change while others struggle with adapting – we try hard to support everyone's journey.

We measure satisfaction through regular surveys to capture data, but also through:

- retention rates – which are significantly higher than the benchmark average for the sector and state

- use of personal leave – this isn't always a good measure as we strongly advocate staff to take time off when they are unwell

- interest in working across sites, special projects and engaging in higher duties

- our success in promoting from within – with staff experiencing the same selection process alongside external candidates

- engagement on our social media sites providing a measure of interaction

- participation and engagement at forums and other staff events

- personal reflection

- appraisals and 360° professional performance reviews

- client feedback on performance and engagement

- how often an employee goes above and beyond their roles – not because they have been asked but because they see an opportunity and a need

- how cohesive the smaller staff groups/teams work together to achieve outcomes for the clients they support.

How do you measure customer satisfaction? What are the key customer data points that providers should be collecting in order to really understand the customer experience?

In the past it's always been about regular face-to-face feedback, surveys and other standardised processes to gather information.

We have established a team specifically to support the 'customer journey' and assigned to develop strong customer relationships as well as implement NDS's Social Impact Measurement Tool (SIMT) to help us to establish a more robust picture of what our customers are feeling and thinking.

We encourage regular reviews of support and services, which include when the client requests one as well as diarised around key dates throughout their NDIS plan.

More recently, a number of service providers have removed the 'team leader' role from their structure to create a direct relationship between the service user and co-ordinator/manager. We opted to retain this integral role as clients have voiced that consistency is key to their services with the team leader creating a lot of this in building, supporting and being present for the team of workers providing support.

This is definitely an area that requires ongoing review to ensure we use the most suitable methods for our clients to provide their feedback.

What role does your CEO play in driving the culture?

Our CEO is integral to the organisation's culture. If the CEO isn't on board, we are at risk of losing a shared vision. The CEO needs to be observed by staff to walk the walk and talk the talk with our CREDIT values front of mind. We are extremely fortunate to have Matt Collins, who has great vision for the organisation, empowering us with 'playing space' to foster innovation, and supporting us with managing change as we enter the new NDIS world. He once was a support worker himself – our staff greatly respect and trust his insight.

We are encouraged to 'call it' with each other when CREDIT isn't being used. We trust this to be handled in a dignified and respectful manner, in keeping with those same values. This same rule applies to the CEO, confronting him if we believe he isn't aligning his thinking and approach with our values (a rare occurrence of course).

We talk about the CEO having a significant role to play, but further to this, our board members are not immune. They too are important champions committed to our CREDIT culture. Again, this is vital in ensuring we as an organisation remain true to our values and remain united in our Vision and Mission.

Chapter 6

Step 3: Recruit for Values

'The best run companies have a very clear understanding of what their culture is and who makes a good a fit. They are relentless about who they let in.'

Simon Sinek

A few months ago, I received an email from a client, the CEO of a disability service organisation. He wanted to discuss the recent hire of a Marketing Manager that went sour: 'I don't know where we went wrong. He came with great experience and fabulous references. But once he was in the job he just could not implement the marketing plan. He couldn't even report on it. I had to let him go.'

I asked him if the candidate was questioned about the actual outcomes of his past campaigns. I asked if other members of the team had the chance to also interview him before he was hired. I asked if he provided any evidence of great people skills or a 'hands-on' approach to project management.

Here was an extremely intelligent, values-driven leader who had approached the hiring process doing 'all the right things'. But here's the catch: values-based recruitment is about looking for evidence of 'the whole person' who will be entering your culture. Have they got the sensitive people skills you're going to need in the role? Do they enjoy being of service, being part of a team, being part of a community?

In a recent chat this same CEO shared the following: 'We over-corporatised the process. In our efforts to implement a professional process, we ticked all the boxes, we did the scenario planning, but what we didn't do was focus on the person. We focused on the VBR model.'

From an outsider's viewpoint there are many theories and practices that complicate HR. The risk is that these frameworks supersede the human element. It's too easy to over intellectualise the hiring process and fail to listen for the values that actually motivate people or 'listen' for the whole person. In the end we're left wondering, *what were we thinking hiring that person?*

Much has already been written about values-based recruitment. So in this chapter, I'd like to briefly touch on the fundamentals with a marketer's lens and then offer some practical insights.

What is values-based recruitment?

Values-based recruitment is about attracting, hiring and retaining people who share the values of the organisation. The term 'values-based recruitment' (VBR) seems to have first been coined by the National Health Service in the UK in response to social care sector reforms.

It's predicated on the belief that you cannot change someone's inherent personal values but you can always build their skills, so it's better to place the emphasis on hiring someone who is a 'values fit' with your organisational culture. Values are the non-negotiable common denominator of every robust, high performance, organisational culture. (NDS has developed an excellent VBR toolkit for service providers who are seeking more information as to how to implement it in their organisations.[26])

---

26   www.nds.org.au/value-based-recruitment.

Clickability is a ratings and review platform for the disability sector that was launched in 2014 by two social workers, Aviva Beecher Kelk and Jenna Moffat. They have a phenomenal staff retention rate and a great workplace culture. In my interview with Aviva, I asked her about why she had been so successful in attracting and retaining great talent:

We make sure that every time we bring somebody on, it is about connecting with your heart and your 'why', not just why does this organisation exist, not just telling a story of the organisation or a story about the founders, but why am I here?

It is no coincidence that the CEOs of Clickability and Fighting Chance made exactly the same comment in their interviews. Both organisations have no trouble finding new staff. Both organisations have a robust and vibrant workplace culture.

As mentioned in the previous chapter, every strong brand is underpinned by values that are 'lived' on a daily basis. Values-based recruitment seeks to tie these values to every step of the recruitment process: how easily the new person fits in, how well they perform, and how long they stay will depend upon their values alignment.

It works both ways

What is often missing from the VBR recruitment framework is the new employee's experience of that process. How was it for them? Have you ever asked your employees about *their* recruitment experience? How well did it reflect the organisation's values? How could you have improved the experience? What's working well and what isn't?

Through a marketer's lens, if we treat the potential new recruits as a key target market then we need to do the firsthand research required to understand their actual 360-degree experience of your organisation. For VBR to be authentic you need to walk your own talk.

Little things mean a lot when it comes to living your values. It is an invaluable exercise to review the recruitment process in light of the actual employee experience. For example, if 'respect' is one of your organisation's values:

- How timely was your response to their first contact?

- How were they greeted when they arrived for the interview or 'open day'?

- Were the bathrooms clean or filled with empty boxes?

- Was there gossipy small talk between staff at your reception?

- Was the interviewer punctual?

If 'inclusion' is one of your values:

- How broadly did you advertise the role? Did you offer it internally? Did you include people without disability qualifications? Did you consider people with diverse life experiences and skillsets?

- Did you offer it to people with disabilities, people from different ethnic backgrounds, different ages and genders?

- Does your process allow for people with different access needs?

- Did you interview one on one, or were others involved in the selection process?

- Were your customers involved in the interview process?

Ironically, through a marketer's lens it sometimes looks like the human element is missing from the VBR process design. Listed below are a few recruiting mistakes I've seen in the last 12 months, all of which reveal something about the actual values driving 'how we do things around here' in the respective organisations. It underlines the importance of living your values when it comes to first impressions. It also underlines the importance of doing the research on your own organisation to find out exactly the sort of 'first impressions' you're actually delivering:

- *'We advertised the job too soon – can you reapply in three months?'* A senior manager shared that he was originally told by the HR Manager that the role he had applied for had simply been advertised too soon. Lucky for the organisation, he was still between roles at the time and was able to wait.

- *'Sorry, but we don't accept CVs at reception; you have to apply online.'* This was the actual response from a provider's receptionist to an extremely high quality candidate seeking to return to work. Would you turn away anyone like this? How institutionalised are your frontline processes?

Case study

The Housing Connection

The Housing Connection (THC) is a Sydney-based disability service provider with a total revenue of $5 million who offer an outstanding customer experience. There are several much larger providers operating within a five-kilometre radius who have lost customers to THC because of this.

Their values are *Social Justice, Passion, Integrity, Social Inclusion, Respect and Effectiveness*. I asked their Client Services Director, Anne Louise Hickey, what her secret was:

> **It's simple – it's the people we hire. This has to be more than a job. It's got to be in your DNA. It has to be something you're passionate about. It's who you are. It's in your blood. We value things like Social Justice, so I tell staff, don't be complacent!**

Attracting 90,000 more

In March 2019, online job ads posted their biggest monthly decline in size in years. This decrease was due to a slump in demand for sales workers, administrative staff and technicians.

At the same time, job advertisements for health and support workers surged 29.4%.[27]

Disability is one of Australia's fastest growing sectors, with an estimated one in five new jobs coming from this sector.[28]

Given that an extra 90,000 workers are required to meet the NDIA's own targets, the question becomes how do we reframe the role of the disability support worker so that it becomes a real alternative for quality jobseekers?

This is not about new position descriptions for existing roles. This is about being prepared to reinvent your organisational structure to ensure that your frontline teams have the support they need to deliver on the changing needs of your customers.

Think customer first, then frontline staff, then rest of organisation, because the entire organisation exists to serve the new key relationship mentioned in chapter 2. Anything else is just a short-term solution that your new recruits will eventually see through.

The values disconnect at the heart of NDIS

Disability workers deserve role clarity and a clear career path. They also deserve the training to do the job they were hired to do; they need professional development and support; they need to be paid appropriately; and they have the right to be mentored and feel safe, valued and supported in the workplace.

---

27 www.abc.net.au/news/2019-04-24/online-job-ads-fall-by-most-in-six-years/11043940.
28 *The Australian Financial Review*, 22 March 2019.

At a systemic level, the NDIS is failing the very people it relies on: the frontline disability support worker. How can we possibly expect a quality service if providers don't have the margin to reinvest in the people expected to deliver their services? This is the 'values disconnect' at the heart of the NDIS. Investment in workforce development is the major building block missing from the NDIA's funding model.

Think local

Your customers must be able to influence recruitment decisions. People with disabilities deserve support workers who match their own needs. This requires a complete rethink about who and how to hire. There are several organisations doing entrepreneurial stuff to attract new talent and greater age, gender, and ethnic diversity into their organisations.

Many providers report that demand far exceeds supply and they struggle to find disability support workers, particularly allied health professionals. This involves recruiting people with the relevant, transferable skills from outside the disability sector.

Marketing, client engagement and business development are examples of the different types of skills needed under the new funding model.

The bottom line is this: you need to go out there to where the talent is, speaking in their language, appealing to their interests and being flexible to their needs. This involves raising your profile within your local community, changing your position descriptions and changing the way you advertise and recruit.

Don't just think of speaking opportunities at TAFE and university open days, think of long-term partnership opportunities with the TAFE and university itself! Or the local gym, local Pilates, or local allied health professional.

Recruitment is now a whole-of-organisation business development function, not just an HR function. Have a look at your nearest tertiary institution; find out if anyone in your networks knows someone. If your competitors don't already have a partnership, then get in there. If your competitors do already have a partnership, get in there anyway and discuss how you could work together to ensure that people with disabilities have greater access to mainstream and specialist quality support services.

Case study

Healthy Change Challenge (HCC)

HCC is a Newcastle and Hunter Region–based social enterprise and health program for people with disabilities and/or mental illness. HCC partner or team up with a number of organisations including the University of Newcastle in the local communities to increase the social engagement and awareness of participants.

When you visit their fresh, engaging website, this is an organisation that knows how to project its values. Their partnership approach to service delivery completely reframes the 'support worker' role, instead providing capacity building coaching to participants and demonstrating their values in action:

> **We have teamed up with the most innovative and engaging people and organisations to create inclusive, capacity building communities. This includes the best trainers, coaches, health professionals and support workers to ensure the quality of the program continues to improve as we grow around Australia.**

Please get in touch if you would like to find
out more about how we roll and operate in our
unique and special way. We are more than happy
to share and work in collaboration to ultimately
make sustainable improvements to the lives of
marginalised people and their support networks.'

Not surprisingly, their team includes many health professionals, university graduates and undergraduates. HCC are always open to collaboration and will soon be sharing everything about how the organisation works on their website (www.healthychangechallenge. com). Coaches and participants also post daily updates of their activities on the Healthy Change Challenge social media platforms Facebook and Instagram.

The 'EVP' and the paradigm shift

The 'employee value proposition' is an HR term that describes 'the unique set of benefits an employee receives in return for the skills, capabilities and experience they bring to a company'.[29]

It usually comprises a basic set of things like pay, training, career path, benefits, and so on. However, from a marketer's viewpoint these components don't necessarily reflect what your employees *really* value about your organisation. This requires internal research.

In this sector, it's most likely to be things like the people they work with, the people they serve, and their ability to make a meaningful, positive difference to someone else's life.

Offering a decent wage, a fair roster, adequate training and a safe, clean workplace is a low benchmark for an organisation that wishes to be seen as genuinely values driven.

This has impacts for the current paradigm shift in the disability sector that gives decision making and funding to the individual

---

29   workology.com/employee-value-propositions-evp.

consumer. This paradigm shift means providers need to rethink their business model, and be far more accountable and values based in their hiring decisions.

The new key relationship (the frontline support worker and customer relationship) means that the employee value proposition should be a mirror of the customer value proposition. The values that underpin your culture will drive the benefits you offer your staff in the same way that they impact the customer experience. Thinking commercially while retaining your core values is one of the biggest challenges for service providers.

For providers like Fighting Chance their culture has become the primary drawcard. They have no problem filling roles thanks to word-of-mouth advertising from their existing staff and families. Their culture has become the primary benefit in their employee value proposition.

'A team is not a group of people who work together. A team is a group of people who trust each other.'

Simon Sinek

Act like an owner

Time and again, when conducting research for this book I came across the phrase 'act like an owner'. It's a phrase more commonly found in the language of small business than in the disability sector. But it's a phrase that deserves more attention.

If the new key relationship is the one between the frontline support worker and the customer, imagine the quality of that relationship if that support worker was empowered to think and act as if the organisation was actually *their* business.

Google is famous for providing the right gimmicks and perks to attract talent. At a media event in 2016 to celebrate Google's 18th birthday, Stacy Sullivan, Google's Chief Culture Officer, revealed that Google had grown up. Their focus was not so much about luring talent and identifying a good cultural fit. They now look for people who share their values and can think like an owner. Their four focus areas when hiring are: skills, critical thinking, leadership and cultural fit. Her advice to other employers included:

When hiring, never let the bar drop in terms of your standards, especially on the culture fit side. Don't hire experts if they are not good for the company. Retention requires good communication and transparency. Bring people 'into the fold' so they are empowered to change things. We want people to think and act like owners, as if this is your company.[30]

Bringing people 'into the fold' requires complete transparency around your business processes and direction. This also requires a strong alignment around core values.

If your employee has the capacity to think like an owner, it can change the whole power structure and communication flow. It basically means they're a problem solver; they act as if *they* are where the buck stops, and you begin to see genuine frontline innovation that is co-designed with the customer.

In 2018, Stanford Brown, a North Sydney–based financial services firm, was voted the 13th best place to work in Australia (in the under 100 employees category). CEO Jonathan Hoyle, speaking at the FPA Conference Professionals Congress, shared that 'we act as if our staff own the company. We employ talented and motivated people. They know what to do, and that's where trust comes in.'[31]

Robyn Kaczmarek, Co-Founder and Co-operative Development Officer at The Co-operative Life, Australia's first worker-owned

---

30   *The Australian*, 2 October 2016.
31   www.moneyandlife.com.au/professionals/focus/4-top-tips-for-building-a-great-culture.

co-operative in social care, shares this approach. For Robyn, getting people to think like an owner is 'the key pin':

> It took me five years to understand that ... It's not that we're a co-operative; it's because we're helping them to think like an owner. I had the idea that ownership was the key factor – that came from the co-operatives. It comes down to the business being owned by the employees.

Sean Dempsey, CEO of Plan Partners, was very specific about the qualities they look for when hiring:

> They have to have resilience; they must be able to cope with some of the very challenging situations that we find our customers living with, and they must have an enormous dose of emotional intelligence and self-awareness.

> They have to also be a problem solver. We often use the phrase, *'We will be part of the solution and will not allow ourselves to be part of a problem'*.

This ability to solve problems, to own an issue, and to act like an owner requires an entirely new approach to the recruiting process. It's not surprising that Plan Partners lists one of their values as: 'We Own It'.

Adopting a brand value that encapsulates this problem-solving ability – this level of personal ownership and accountability – will actually enable your employees to more easily adapt to change, provided they are also entrusted with the freedom to respond.

VBR resources

Consistency, authenticity and integrity are key to creating any values-based recruitment process. Every organisation will have a different set of values that it seeks to bring alive.

I'm not an HR expert or an organisational psychologist, however I can offer you a few examples of organisations that have used values-based recruitment with outstanding results:

- **Helen Sanderson of Wellbeing Teams UK** has completed outstanding work in the area of self-organising teams and developing further the work of Frederic Laloux in his wonderful book *Reinventing Organisations.*[32] You will find more about her work at http://helensandersonassociates.co.uk/person-centred-practice/

- **Nikki Gatenby of Propellernet UK.** Her advertising agency only ever has 60 employees! At Propellernet, the employees are their biggest ambassadors, living their values and delivering an extremely healthy commercial return. It's a culture focused on enabling every employee to fulfil their potential (and their dreams!): 'For our values to have real impact, they have to be living, breathing drivers of behaviour. And the way we make that happen is by putting them front and centre from day one. Or indeed, from day minus-one, by incorporating them into our interview process.'[33]

- **Southwest Airlines US** receives a new job application every two seconds and less than 2% of all applicants are hired. They are very clear about hiring not for skills but for values or 'attributes', and use behavioural interview questions to determine whether applicants have those values. Everything they do, such as how they hire, how they conduct professional development and how they promote, is tied to their organisation's values. In 2014, 75% of their employees described their job as 'a calling'.

---

32 Frederic Laloux, *Reinventing Organisations*, Nelson Parker, 2014.
33 *Superengaged: How to transform business performance by putting people and purpose first*, Nikki Gatenby, 2019.

Their values are:

▸ A servant's heart (the ability to put others first, treat everyone with respect and proactively be of service).

▸ A warrior spirit (a desire to excel, act with courage, persevere and innovate).

▸ A fun-loving attitude (passion, joy and an aversion to taking oneself too seriously).[34]

- **The Ritz-Carlton Hotel Company.** The Ritz-Carlton is considered the gold standard in developing the customer service experience, and it begins with the people they hire. Their hiring process sets the tone for the pride their employees take in their work. As Tony Mira, a General Manager at Ritz Carlton, puts it: 'You can't help but feel special whether you're a leader or a frontline employee, when people take so much time to get to know you and afterward deem you acceptable.'[35]

---

34 'How Southwest Airlines Hires Such Dedicated People', Julie Weber, *Harvard Business Review*, 2 December 2015.

35 Joseph A. Michelli, *The New Gold Standard: 5 leadership principles for creating a legendary customer experience*, McGraw Hill, 2008.

Summary

▶ Values-based recruitment (VBR) is about attracting, hiring and retaining people who share the values of the organisation.

▶ People bring their whole self to work, not just a 'work self'.

▶ VBR works both ways. It requires the organisation to 'walk their talk'.

▶ Recruitment is a whole-of-organisation business development function.

▶ A strong culture is a primary drawcard for future talent.

▶ The employee value proposition should mirror your customer value proposition.

▶ 'Act like an owner' or 'accountability' is an essential value for a resilient culture.

Interview

Aviva Beecher Kelk, Co-Founder, Clickability

Aviva Beecher Kelk is Co-Founder and CEO of Clickability, a rating and review 'Trip Advisor' type of service for the disability sector which was launched in 2014 in response to the distinct lack of quality information available. Her team's goal is to provide a platform through which the disability community can obtain reliable information about support services in order to make informed choices and decisions. Aviva is a social worker and a PhD student with a background in mental health, community development and project management.

What do you think are the biggest challenges facing the disability sector right now?

I think that looking at the NDIS one of the biggest issues is the workforce. There aren't enough people providing services, and there's really low utilisation of staff in a lot of agencies. We get phone calls every day from people looking for services, and we are consistently hearing that people cannot find suitable support workers or allied health services.

A mother called the other day and she said she had quit her job because she couldn't work and find a support worker for her son at the same time; it was too much. There are a lot of providers who have closed their doors, or they are not taking in new participants because there is just not the workforce there. And others who are at risk of closing because they have staff, but are losing money and not meeting demand because they struggle to efficiently allocate the right staff to the right customers. So that's a real problem.

And the other thing is that people are struggling to find services. So part of it is because the workforce isn't there but the other part is because it's difficult finding services available. There is just a lack of data. Even with the thousands of registered service providers that the NDIS tells us there are in their quarterly reports, only 50% of them are actually putting claims through.

It often takes us several phone calls to make a good referral (of a service for a participant). I don't know if we can extrapolate that or not. Finding out who are the quality providers in a region and then whether they have staff who can provide support to a new participant can be very difficult.

That brings me to my next point: the NDIS industry is not good at using data and technology effectively. I still get excited when providers tell me they are investing in a CRM! There is just so much fabulous technology out there to help with utilisation of resources and a bunch of really cool Internet of Things stuff that has been invented that could have amazing potential.

When we start to talk about technology and the disability sector I think the thing that is going to make the biggest difference to human rights is:

- internet access for everyone will make a huge difference for remote and rural communities

- simple software that ensures that what we are doing, we are doing well. That we are listening to our customers, that we are communicating with them and that we are providing a service that is of a high enough quality that it works for everyone, and that we're properly utilising our existing workforce. Not just a compliant service but a service that actually meets consumer needs and leverages the resources on hand.

So, your one key message for providers on the back of that?

My key message for providers is probably still consistent with what it was a few years ago:

> **To be really clear about the way they communicate what they do, about what makes them unique and**

> about what they can't do. To manage customer
> expectations and only say yes to customers
> that they know that they can support.

I would also say to invest in training people in how to better leverage their technology, and investing in packages that will improve their operations. It really does seem hard to make the change in creating new systems, but that is the only way forward. You can't scale and you can't offer a great service when everything is being done manually.

What role is Clickability playing now in the sector?

We play a *TripAdvisor* type role of letting customers and families share reviews with each other. We have a list of services that are available that are essentially sorted by who has the most reviews.

We get a lot of phone calls and emails from families, Local Area Co-ordinators and support co-ordinators asking us to help them find services for participants, and we help match consumers to services.

We also do capacity building work with providers on their marketing. I see that role as being a really key piece of the concept of *market stewardship*. Markets and welfare are not easy bedfellows. It is really difficult to make a market work at all, let alone in a way that promotes human rights. We can see there is a workforce shortage as supply doesn't meet the demand. All of those things need to be nursed, they need to have stewardship around them to make sure that the market works and I see Clickability playing a role in that.

What are the customer data points that service providers should be monitoring to really understand that participant experience?

The key data points that have come out for us when we have done an analysis of our reviews on Clickability are around outcomes, customer service and staff. In the last two years the most critical comments have been around the availability and consistency of staff.

Seeing how the market is affecting the customer experience is so interesting.

When I say 'customer service', I'm talking about communication. (Answering phone calls and emails. If you can't answer the phone then have voicemail. Not everyone does!) If you don't have a website, make sure there is a way for the customer to find and contact you. And managing expectations and having transparency around the customer journey is really important.

How could providers better support their workplace culture?

There is a lot of evidence about what makes people happy in their workplace. Employees want to be paid, challenged, acknowledged and all these sorts of things. Making sure there is good training and good supervision is important in this sector too, because some of the work that people do is really emotionally and physically challenging, and when they haven't had a background in this field it can be really hard. Making sure staff are feeling confident, thinking about management as a coaching opportunity.

I come from a social work background where we are all about supervision. We ask questions to prompt critical reflection, like, *how was that for you? How can you do better next time? What support do you need?* We have a really small team at Clickability and part of what we do is foster leadership in small and big ways. *Yes there is a problem, so how do you think we should solve it?* Or, if there is a meeting, asking who would like to run it. Generally fostering a culture of sharing responsibility for where we are going.

The other way to support workplace culture is being generous with praise, and very clear with KPIs and expectations with staff as much as with customers.

The other big thing is making sure that we are clear on our culture, on our tone and on our identity. We did this nice exercise a few years back: we were taking first steps in designing some comms and marketing and we ended up writing a manifesto. What flowed off the back of that was discussion around how we communicate a tone that is consistent across all of us.

Having a consistent tone of the culture is also about making sure that staff can connect with their hearts in what they are doing so that delivering a service is not just a compliance exercise. There is such a beautiful opportunity in this sector to understand the impact you are having. For example, *how is what I am doing impacting the organisation and impacting this individual? How can I have that in my heart and not just turn up for work?*

Do you have anything else to add?

The only thing I would add to that is that our culture is really front and centre. We make sure that every time we bring somebody on, it is about connecting with your heart and your 'why' – not just why does this organisation exist, not just telling a story of the organisation or a story about the founders, but why am *I* here?

It's about making sure that as a team we are really connected with our *why*, with our *mission* and with the *ethics* of where we are going – and that plays out through keeping clear on our change logic. When we are thinking about changing what we do, first being clear on where we are going and why.

How do you attract talent at Clickability?

We have a small team. We have phenomenal retention, and when we find somebody, we hold onto them and we offer them coaching and professional development opportunities. We make an effort for it to be a really great workplace. Our team are quite separate; some people are in Melbourne, NSW, Brisbane, so we find ways of using technology to ensure that we continue to feel close.

The other half of my answer is that we have really made sure that all of our 'hires' have come from the community so they connect with our mission. That means a lot of people with disability, and a lot of parents of kids with disability and people who have worked in other roles in the industry.

As CEO and co-founder, what role do you play in driving culture?

I feel that it's my role and my honour to embody it and to set a tone of it, to lead by example, because culture is everything.

If our culture is not right, if we are not communicating well, then our operations are not going to work so smoothly. If our customer service team is feeling burnt out, our customers are going to have a bad experience and our customer retention is going to decrease.

So how does this work on a daily basis? It is everything from how we dress, to where we work, to the way that we communicate with each other, the way we set up our systems, the way we solve problems, the way that we encourage leadership, the way we use points of tension or conflict to raise new points of view. It's about empathy and compassion but also about clarity and boundaries.

I think it is important to think holistically. It feels easier to change a process than it does to challenge culture, but it is no different. If you want to change a process you need to do the training, and if you want to change the culture you need to do the training as well – it is about moulding relationships rather than moulding systems.

We are not robots. We are in social services because we like people and usually not because we like systems. Thinking of a person as an ecosystem (a social worker metaphor) not just as a person is quite useful. So, the domains of their life – their social life, their financial life, their religious life, their friends and whatever else – and how they all interrelate. The person is not autonomous, ever, in a social work paradigm. The same goes for an organisation.

Interview

Nicola Hayhoe, CEO, The Housing Connection

In 1981, a group of parents who were concerned about the future accommodation for adults with intellectual disability formed an action group in the northern Sydney region. They formed The Housing Connection (THC), an organisation which today supports over 200 adults with intellectual and other disabilities to live meaningful, inclusive and valued lives. The organisation excels in one-to-one support, transitioning people from high-support environments into more independent living. Nicola Hayhoe has been CEO for three years and has worked in the sector for the last 25 years.

What role does culture play at The Housing Connection? How do you keep your values front of mind for your teams, Nicola?

Initially it all goes back to our values-based recruitment. The big part of what we do is look for staff who actually have the values and share the vision and the mission of the organisation. Because if you don't have that initially it is hard to build.

Then, through our induction training process, through to being allocated to a team leader, through to their orientation working with specific clients and their role as part of a team, the focus is always on 'how we do things at The Housing Connection'.

So, what does that look like? Making ourselves accessible, approachable, being respectful. It is demonstrating the organisation's values in practice – how we engage with each other, how we set those expectations, when people walk in the door and on an ongoing basis.

It needs to happen across the organisation, both vertically and horizontally. That can sometimes be a challenge particularly if you have new directors, or new managers or personnel.

That is one of the challenges, finding out when someone is not operating in line with the mission or values, or finding out that people don't understand what this means in practice. Sometimes you can have that disconnect.

Is there a procedure that you follow to tie the values to daily practice? It is the culture at The Housing Connection that really makes it a standout for me and a lot of organisations struggle to maintain that link.

I think it is about the leadership, supervision, mentoring and support across all levels. Whether it's the interactions with our Manager, Client Services, Anne Louise or myself or the team leaders or other team members. It really relies on the leadership at every level actually facilitating, demonstrating 'how we do things at The Housing Connection' – and what that means in practice.

When we talk about person-centred human resource management you have to be able to demonstrate that. You can't all of a sudden become an organisation that is all about respect and then treat people really poorly. It is all about actually how you walk the talk in different areas, delivering services, supervision, support; whatever it might happen to be. It is following those values through into action in everything you do.

You are a small organisation and communication is very flat; does that organisational structure impact your culture?

I think the value of being a small organisation is that you have those touch points. I would know most of the staff; I know most of the clients. Having that means that there is a direct kind of linkage across the organisation. I think it is much easier for us, as a small organisation, to have that reach, to have that visibility and to have that impact. It is much harder for larger organisations that operate more like a corporate entity to achieve that level of congruence throughout their organisation.

Did you change your organisational structure to better support your culture and your customer experience?

We have made some changes over the last three years, but some key fundamentals remained the same. Our structure is an ongoing piece that is reviewed based on our growth and our capacity at any given point in time. We've created some flexibility in our structure to hopefully be nimble to changes, while reducing our overhead costs by changing some functions.

We are leaner in our overheads. It is very much a fine line under NDIS because of the resourcing issues around the pricing. Our focus has very much been to put resources into our frontline, the people doing the direct support. We still have a lot of work to do.

We are reviewing our induction and training processes because we know we can't afford *not* to train our staff to the level of our expectations. We are reviewing *how* we can do that cost effectively to ensure that we maintain the quality of our service delivery. That's a big challenge.

Have you changed your induction and performance management to reflect your values and support your culture?

It is a work in progress. We have reviewed and revamped our induction process and we are looking to roll out a very different way of how we support and mentor our staff. In some ways we haven't fundamentally changed how we train and resource staff. Our focus has always been to provide resourcing, support and training and commitment to our frontline staff.

In terms of attracting future talent, are you struggling with that or are you finding it is coming through word of mouth?

We seem to be constantly recruiting. Trying to find the calibre of staff has been a challenge. We don't necessarily look inside the sector. That is really again about coming back to the values, sharing the values and the ethos and outlook, that is critically important;

everything else we think that we can train. We get a lot of word-of-mouth referrals and we primarily advertise through Care Careers, Ethical Jobs and Seek.

We also have staff referral incentive in place. If an employee refers someone to us who goes on to become a new team member staying beyond the six-month period, we offer a $500 referral gift certificate for those staff members who are finding great people in their networks for us. This incentive has been working really well – word of mouth has been really important for us.

What do you think are the key employee data points that providers should be collecting to really understand the employee experience?

We do things like celebrating birthdays, having a birthday cake, having a dinner out periodically within teams. We have lots of BBQs with the people we support, their families and our staff. Our social experiences become an opportunity for everyone to get together. Our end-of-year celebrations, again they tend to be both for people we support, their families and other community members and staff. We like to celebrate achievements and milestones.

What sort of things should people be looking for to determine if they have a healthy culture or not? Staff satisfaction is only one very linear way.

Obviously some key things that come back in the sector are having an appropriate career path and having appropriate remuneration. Some of the key reasons people leave the organisation are out of our control.

We have had a couple of people recently who we identified as talent that we promoted in the organisation and developed them into more senior roles. Eventually they left the organisation because they didn't see that there was a career path that would support them to earn more money. They were able to get more money in the public sector. Even though we pay them appropriately what we can, it still may not be enough in terms of competing.

What role do you feel the CEO has to play in driving culture and what role you do play at the Housing Connection?

My role is strategic planning and then translating that into operational plans. That includes a consideration of how we continue to maintain our values, our culture and our staff. It's about that vertical and horizontal integration.

Having new directors or new boards can be a real tipping point, or it has been in the past. It can be seen as a real risk for our culture. It's my role to make sure there is alignment for our mission, purpose and values at the board level and that this translates into strategic planning which translates into operational planning. Having that framework to carry through the organisation in everything we do.

Do you currently measure customer satisfaction, client satisfaction?

Yes, we have been undertaking a survey every three years via Voice at Macquarie University. We have a survey that goes out to people we support, their family members/nominee, and also to staff. In between this there is ongoing dialogue with clients, families and staff. Our strategic plan for 2019 includes some additional consideration as to how we engage with stakeholders.

Did you feel that was an adequate measure of customer experience for you?

I'm fairly confident because we have our compliments/complaints register and we get a lot of feedback informally through conversations that we have with our staff, or through parents or people we support. We get a lot of positive feedback and I think that we are fairly quickly able to address anything that we think is an issue, so overall we have a very high level of satisfaction.

You have really excelled in that transitioning people into independent living, haven't you?

Yes. That has historically been one of our strengths; one of our founding services was actually transitioning people from high-support environments – either institutions or family homes – into more independent living. Focusing on building skills and capacity to live as independently as possible.

Chapter 7 ▶

Step 4: Understand Your Current Culture

'Always treat your employees exactly as you want them to treat your best customers.'

Steven Covey

Okay, so let's imagine that you've just recruited for a new middle-management position. You've found someone fired up with enthusiasm, with fabulous experience, and he is a genuine 'values fit' for your organisation. Let's call him Tony.

In his first few weeks, Tony will begin to discover 'how things are really done around here'. If he's surrounded by a supportive team who shares his values and his drive to achieve, then it goes without saying that Tony will be more likely to thrive and perform.

If Tony walks into the office every day only to be surrounded by staff who are stressed, late, sick (again), staff who bring problems without suggested solutions, or an entire team who simply feel overwhelmed, how long is his enthusiasm likely to last?

Take the simple example of the new disability support worker (Kate) who is always punctual. She starts work at a new organisation. At her job interview she was told, 'We really value punctuality here so you're going to totally fit in.'

Kate starts work … and guess what? It seems that everyone in the organisation runs at least five minutes late – for everything. What happens? After a few weeks, Kate is also running five minutes late – for everything. Because the actual, unspoken organisational behaviour pattern is: 'Nobody really runs on time around here. Take a chill pill.'

Patterns of thinking drive patterns of behaviour

These patterns of behaviour are driven by shared patterns of thinking.

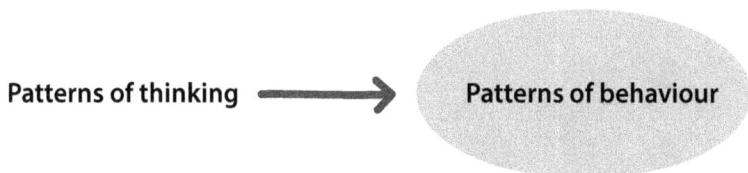

Patterns of thinking ⟶ **Patterns of behaviour**

Patterns of thinking lie at the heart of workplace culture; they act as a filter influencing collective actions. We can only begin to address these behaviours when we recognise and address the thinking that produces them.

This is why workplace cultures can be so hard to change. This is why it sometimes feels like some enormous inertia is at play. It's like the elephant on the table that nobody is talking about, because they haven't identified it. They know there's something big and heavy staring at them but they're just not sure what it is.

In the previous example I used punctuality because it's easy to witness and measure.

It might sound pedantic, but let's be honest, five minutes late is still late. That's the level of honesty you need if you're serious about addressing your culture. You *will* sound pedantic. You *will* drive some people nuts at first. But building a healthy, robust culture requires action. Consistent, visible action.

Understanding your culture

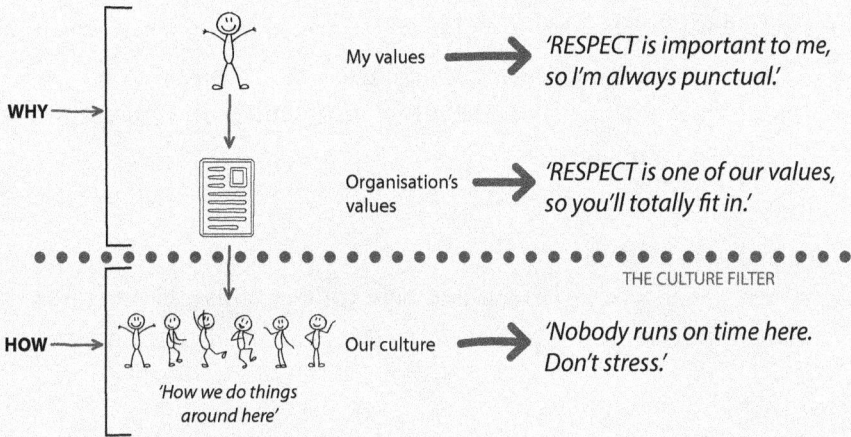

'How we do things around here.'

If you say you value punctuality, you're actually saying you value *respect* – and you have to demonstrate that consistently. Keep it simple. Walk the talk. Do what you say you will do. This is not rocket science. This is about remembering that people bring their whole selves to work, not just their work self.

Here are some examples of actual thinking patterns I have found embedded within the workplace of many disability and aged-care organisations:

- *'I'm just too busy'*, or, *'We're just too busy'*. Of course you are, but notice if this is the same excuse that comes up every time there is poor performance. You may have a deeper cultural issue than you realise.

- *'Nobody speaks up.'* If you say you value honest communication, where is the honesty in allowing someone to totally burn out or allowing poor behaviour to go ignored?

- *'The therapists don't talk to us.'* If you say you value teamwork, how well do your therapists and support workers communicate with each other?

- *'Our admin staff are the most change resistant.'* If you say you value trust and understanding, how many times do your admin staff visit your sites?

The cultural filter

How others collectively behave and how your systems and processes reinforce those behaviours create 'how things are really done around here'.

Actual customer experience

Workplace cultural filter

Employee's values

Our behaviours are influenced by the behaviour patterns of the people we work with. This is the reason that culture can be so hard to shift.

I used to think that if you recruited for values that you could automatically unlock an unbeatable customer experience. But from years of listening to the actual customer experience I now know this isn't the case.

Because we are 'tribal beings', our thoughts and behaviours are influenced by the stories and actions of those around us.

These behaviour patterns create what I call a 'cultural filter'. This filter will influence every employee's daily interactions with each other and with your customers – creating the actual customer experience. This 'filter' can have a positive or a negative influence. Often there are sub-cultures within organisations, each with a different cultural filter.

'One Team. One Dream' is the actual mantra of an extraordinary out-of-home care children's emergency support team operated by Westhaven in central NSW under the leadership of Cath Deveigne, General Manager of Children's Services. Westhaven has continued to grow, due to the team's resilience and skills they are able to support children and young people with significant disabilities. Everyone in her team has each other's support to deliver a quality service that enables children and young people to achieve their goals. They are beyond dedicated and passionate about their work.

How to assess your existing culture

Before you can begin to change your culture, you need to observe, understand and 'own' your existing culture – and then get your team to do the same! (That's the really hard bit, but we'll get to that.)

It's a tough gig for a CEO. If you can't honestly acknowledge the cultural stressors operating within your organisation then your employees won't believe you're serious about genuine culture change. There are certainly tools such as voice surveys and staff engagement available on the market. But these tools should never replace your own personal fact-finding mission. This involves empathy, time and genuine curiosity.

Empathy requires that you take the time to really listen and 'tune in' to someone else. It's not a transactional skill, it's a listening skill. In my experience, it doesn't come naturally for everyone. However, if you can begin to actually feel what your employees feel and feel what your customers feel, then you can begin to understand what's really going on in your workplace culture on an entirely new level. This is not a black-and-white report conducted annually; successful cultural change requires a *personal* daily commitment to creating a great place to work.

'It will be our staff who make us or break us; how you deliver services is key.'

Marketing Manager Disability Provider, SA

You also need to be genuinely curious. When I first start working with a new organisation, whether it's for a marketing strategy program or a cultural change program, I begin by meeting one on one with people from every layer of the organisation. I call this 'background research and consultation', but it just means I take the time to be genuinely curious. This prevents me from jumping to conclusions or assuming that one person's version of what's required is the only version.

Stress kills curiosity. It's exactly this type of proactive, objective listening that enables you to not only uncover the hidden patterns driving organisational culture but identify those golden opportunities for incremental, leading-edge innovation.

Some consultants call this 'management by walking around' (MBWA). It appears as if it's a random stroll, but it's far more than that. It's an opportunity to build trust, and nothing builds trust faster than honest, face-to-face communication, whether it's with customers or employees.

But let's be clear. You're there to listen for ideas and issues, praise what's right, and to make a real connection. This cannot look like you're simply ticking the box of 'being a good CEO this week'. This is about observing what's really going on and focusing on actual behaviours, and spending genuine time with your people.

When talking to your employees, don't dive into talking about the work; make a human connection. Your first priority is to build trust and then recognise what's working.

Getting under the skin

This list is not meant to overwhelm you, but to just provide some ideas as to how you can get 'under the skin' of the actual culture operating in your organisation:

1. **Observe** what's really going on. Imagine you were applying for the role of CEO of your own organisation and you had the opportunity to visit every site before you decided whether to proceed. This involves actually visiting every site and looking for clues as to how things are operating. How messy are the offices? Are the loos filled with empty boxes? How clear and well-lit are the passageways? Are there any plants or flowers? Is there music? How welcoming does the reception really feel? Are the offices and client areas sterile or engaging? Does it feel like a community works here? Are there family photos? What is on display? Do employees know how to talk about your organisation at a social occasion? How much space is given to whom in the office set up? Are there celebration or achievement awards up on notice boards? Is there a weekly update? Is the organisation's history on display anywhere? Does it look as if that history is actually of any relevance to the employees who walk past it every day? Have you rung

your head office contact number and counted how long it takes for the phone to be answered? Have you sat next to your staff in the customer enquiries area and taken the inbound calls and complaints? Have you sent an email enquiry to your organisation (not from your own email address) and observed the response? (How long did it take, how well did they handle the enquiry, and what did it say about your organisation and how it made you feel?) Have someone you trust apply for a job and see how well their application is handled.

In retail, these practices are called 'comparison shopping your own organisation'. It's one thing to pay a fortune to a consultant to do this for you. But you will really 'get' the impact of your culture if you try it for yourself.

2. **Listen** *for* people, not just *to* people. Listening for people is about active listening for the person behind the content of their conversation. This also concerns how meetings are conducted. It's about listening for the stories people tell, it's about informal one-on-one conversations at every level of the organisation. It's also about knowing the questions to ask and knowing when to stop talking and listen. It's about checking the exit interview results, and checking in with employees after their first day, their first week and their first three months. (Before people will open up in a one-on-one conversation you need to frame the conversation so they feel safe to do so. Framing is an invaluable skill that can be easily taught. I cover it briefly in my Culture Masterclass, and my business now provides several organisations with one-on-one coaching support. Framing is the secret to effective performance-based conversations.)

Ask your employees open-ended questions such as:

▸ What's the toughest part of your day (or your role)?

▶ Where did our induction process (or performance review, or anything recent and relevant) fall down for you – or was it a positive experience?

▶ What's frustrating our customers?

▶ What's frustrating your team?

3. **Check the tech.** Notice how people use technology. Notice how people generally interact with the software and technology in your workplace. These processes and devices often reinforce the existing culture. For example, if your managers rely on email and project planning software for 90% of their communications, chances are you have a culture that is more focused on processes than outcomes. An early warning sign of this is an apparent lack of clear task ownership and projects which are rarely finished. Sound familiar?

Identifying your cultural stress points

Once you have done your own firsthand review, you'll have a fair idea of what's working and what isn't working. You will also have a fair idea of the major internal cultural stressors – those situations or periods during which your employees are feeling particularly frustrated, unheard, abandoned or even unsafe.

These have to be identified before you can get anywhere. Essentially you need a respectful, permission-based, values-driven approach that makes it 'safe' for people to communicate honestly about 'what's really happening'.

What follows may sound like a sales spiel. I don't mean it to be. I just want to explain how, with external facilitation, you can 'safely' get to the heart of what's happening within your workplace culture without isolating or threatening people.

I initially developed my approach back in 2017 in conjunction with a large statewide disability organisation who was struggling with their team's 'personal ownership' of their brand. Thanks to the input from every organisation I've worked with since that time, I'm proud to say that this approach has now evolved into a robust and scalable program for addressing workplace culture called 'Bringing the Brand Alive'.

The Culture Masterclass is a one-day 'train the trainer' version of this model. It trains people in how to implement exercises to successfully shift negative culture in their own organisations. I run it for groups of organisations and as in-house training.

However, when it's run in-house for a single organisation it is particularly powerful. Attendees are selected from across functional areas and hierarchical layers to drive collaboration. The exercises comprise a mix of basic marketing tools which are more commonly used to understand the customer experience, the difference being that we are now actively applying them to the employee experience and measuring the outcomes.

One of the exercises in particular always serves to flush out the major cultural stress points in the workplace.

Visually, it couldn't be simpler. Because it's so highly visual, most attendees quickly 'see' the key cultural stress points operating in their organisation and often in their own teams. And every time I run it, it's a revelation.

Keeping things positive, I call these stress points 'transition points'. As soon as these transition points are acknowledged by the CEO you can usually feel the energy in the room change.

Thanks to feedback from several organisations over the last year, I've found that in each case (while it varied by organisation), within each organisation there was often a single overarching cultural pattern causing every one of those transition points.

Once the team 'sees' this pattern of thinking, each of those transition points can be addressed via a basic 'Culture Action Plan', which is then shared for the input and 'ownership' of the broader organisation.

Shadow shifts: A key transition point

One common stress or transition point that appears in almost every Culture Masterclass is the period of 'shadow shifts'. This is the practice of providing a buddy for a new recruit who 'shadows' them at their place of work, providing training, support and valuable mentoring.

This is a really interesting transition point because it highlights:

- how language indicates the actual culture operating
- how the NDIA's pricing undermines a quality customer experience
- how the NDIA's pricing undermines a values-driven employee experience.

I'd like to make this a bit more personal, because you need to feel the values disconnect here at a personal level to feel the scale of stress imposed on the typical new disability support worker.

Imagine that your 23-year-old, enthusiastic, talented daughter has just started a new job as a disability support worker. The first client she will be working with one on one for three days per week is a 24-year-old man (let's call him Nathan) who is manic depressive, schizophrenic, and has complex behaviour support needs. He also weighs 130 kilos.

Under the previous block funding model, your daughter would have had a more senior support worker with her for the first few weeks until she could confidently and competently handle her client's needs and deliver a quality support service. Under the NDIS Price Guide 2019–20, '… the provider may claim for up to six hours of weekday support per year.' Your daughter would be lucky to have more than one hour of that support.

This raises a series of questions: is this reasonable, or even safe? Is this in her or Nathan's best interests? How can we reasonably overlay a model of quality and clinical governance with this pricing structure?

As a CEO, how can you say you stand for values such as empowerment, compassion or respect if this is the way your organisation is treating its frontline recruits? How long do you think they will stay in that job?

Summary

▶ Collective patterns of thinking drive collective patterns of behaviour.

▶ Patterns of behaviour act as a cultural filter, directly influencing the employee and customer experience.

▶ You need to honestly assess and understand your existing workplace culture before you can change it.

▶ Assessing your culture involves observing actual behaviours and the workplace environment, listening for the person behind the content and noticing how people interact with their technology.

▶ Accurate assessment requires empathy, genuine curiosity and time. It requires empathy, genuine curiosity and time.

▶ You need to identify and understand the key cultural stress points in your workplace before you can create an effective Culture Action Plan.

Interview

Michael Chester, Head of Service Operations, UnitingCare West

UnitingCare West (UCW) provides targeted and integrated services focused on delivering local solutions to local communities, serving over 30,000 West Australians each year. Their programs span the areas of community and family services, disabilities and youth, mental health, independent living and accommodation services. WA is one of the last states to roll out the NDIS, transferring existing WA NDIS funding to the Scheme from April 2018, with full transition of the remainder of disability and mental health services in the period leading up to July 2020. Michael Chester has been with UCW since late 2017. Prior to this, he was Executive Operations Manager with Interchange WA for four years and before that worked in management consulting for more than a decade. Under Michael's guidance, the individualised services team at UnitingCare West is focused on delivering contemporary, individualised approaches to support people to belong and thrive in their community. Recently, he also played a key role reporting to the Commonwealth Government on the impact the WA NDIS decision is having on the disability services sector and the people that the NDIS is intended to support.

What do you think are the biggest challenges facing the disability/ social care sector now? If you had one key message for the sector right now what would it be?

There are three major challenges.

The first is one that's been talked about endlessly, being the viability of some service models and specifically one-to-one community inclusion support within the NDIS pricing framework. In addition to the disconnect with the true cost of support worker wages, this includes the consideration for transport options for people with disability: the NDIS assumes that people with disability will access public transport but the planning process fails to take into account the additional time required to undertake activities when relying on public transport. The onus is put back on service providers to fund fleet capital costs and participants will end up losing out when current fleets reach end-of-life.

Secondly, sourcing and retaining support workers is a really significant issue that's been highlighted for years in the Productivity Commission reports, labour reports, and in the work that National Disability Services (NDS) is doing. The factors that are influencing this include a relatively low unemployment rate; the casualised nature of an NDIS workforce that's impacting the commitment and the retention of support workers; and the comparatively low rates of pay relative to the aptitude and capability we must expect from a workforce working with vulnerable individuals.

The third challenge is the ability to deliver quality services.

In order to deliver quality services, we need the time to develop a skilled workforce, to provide them with the training and education that they need to prepare for getting to know someone and their specific requirements for service delivery on the day – and everything is conspiring against that. The amount of time that can be allocated to training is unrealistic. The casualisation and the consequent turnover of the workforce means we must continually re-train, re-educate, re-inform. So we've got lots of factors impacting on the ability of organisations with any sort of legacy model to deliver quality support viably.

Some of the new models to their credit are very streamlined and very technology driven. That's great. But it's a transactional approach, and I think we're going to see more compliance-driven support rather than quality-driven support.

So, encapsulating all of that I think my key message for the sector concerns our ability as providers to continue to deliver quality services. Considering the impact of the NDIS pricing, workforce skills and retention – it's a real challenge. We want to be delivering quality support rather than just 'attendant care'. But the reality is that some services will be driven by compliance rather than quality.

As a sector we must be lobbying for more realistic pricing arrangements – making it clear that this is not because of self-interest, it is due to the fact that the people we support deserve quality services that enhance their lives rather than just provide transactional assistance.

One only has to look at the modelling around one-to-one community inclusion and realise that there would be few viable businesses in Australia that would be likely to meet the margins and assumptions that have been built into that NDIA pricing model.

How do you address the issue of attracting future staff and retaining quality people at UnitingCare West? Do you necessarily look for disability or human services experience?

This is work in progress for us. Using the NDS Workforce Wizard we were shocked to discover just how casualised our disability workforce is. One of our challenges is that we are a very diverse community service organisation and a lot of our data cuts across many different workforce models and requirements.

Our first step is to make a commitment that we can offer permanent part-time contracts offering minimum hours that we know we can provide to someone and also using that workforce to cover the casual rostering hours that arise when people are sick or on leave. Having a permanent workforce rather than a casual one is much better for the people we support because we can guarantee them some consistency. It's also better for us from a cost perspective in terms of being able to train, educate and inform our support workers to achieve the quality standards that we expect. And by having permanent employees, we're able to mitigate turnover.

But what is really important for us at UCW is that we don't want to create a class of working poor as a consequence of our own employment practices. As we assess the impact of the NDIS on our workforce modelling, the conversation that we're having on a regular basis is: 'What can we do to prevent ourselves falling into the trap of creating a class of working poor?'

What role does your culture play at UnitingCare West? How important is it? How do you keep your values 'front of mind' for your workforce?

As an agency of the Uniting Church, our foundation invites us to create an inclusive, connected and just world. This solid foundation is reinforced by the values we share and how we put those values into action at every opportunity. One of the conversations I have with our frontline support teams as we transition people to the NDIS is that they will be crucial in offering a more autonomous level of support. The policies and procedures manual is not going to be stored in their head every time they're out in the community providing support. So if something happens and they need to react, I reinforce to them that their behaviour should come from a place of values – UCW's values and their own values – as the criteria for making decisions at that critical point in time. If they do that, I will support their decision.

Our values are Empathy, Respect, Inclusiveness, Integrity and Commitment. Our actions and behaviours need to reflect these values each and every day. We have an intranet hub where we publish stories to update the entire team about the work that their colleagues are undertaking and these stories reinforce our values. It's something we take very seriously. When the behaviours or actions of a team member don't reflect our values in action, we can address this as part of the performance development process.

Can you give me a brief outline of your organisational structure and the thinking behind it? In your experience, how is workplace culture impacted by organisational structure?

There's lots going on here! At a broad level, across the whole organisation we've being undergoing a journey of renewal since 2017. This journey is based around the principle of having a radically person-centred approach with every individual that we support across all our community services. So we're breaking down the silos. We're breaking down the idea of putting people into a box that is linked to a program that is linked to specific funding. When a person walks through our door seeking assistance, we ask, 'What are your needs?' and 'How can we meet those needs?'

An element of our renewal journey is adopting the concept and practice of self-organising teams, based on the work of Frederic Laloux. This fits very well into the NDIS model. As I said earlier, we are very conscious that we've had over-casualisation of the disability workforce. Permanency is a critical part of self-organising teams.

Another complication in terms of the transformation of our programs to the NDIS is that we have a number of different programs, funding models and different funders all transitioning at the same time. We have a significant Home & Community Care Program (HACC) for centre-based day-care support in three locations that are not co-located with primary locations. So we're having to educate, inform our support workers and the people we support about the way we will be delivering community access and inclusion services in the future. The transition is very challenging for everybody involved.

We also have a Personal Helpers and Mentors (PHaMs) Program so we're supporting people with mental illness with their access requests to the NDIS. That workforce is permanent full time and does not fit into our NDIS model. We're not sure if we're going to deliver psychosocial disability support because of the challenges of the attendant care pricing model and the expectations of people around the way support is delivered. Coming up with a viable model for that is a major challenge.

We then have the 'standard' models of disability support: supported accommodation, shared living and community inclusion.

So what we're doing with the workforce is working towards a broad-based individualised services workforce rather than a workforce that's sequestered into program-specific areas; a workforce with decentralised decision making, local hubs and a mixture of skillsets.

While we have all these challenges we also have this incredible opportunity to benefit from the different skills this brings. For example, there's a reasonable co-morbidity of people with disability and mental health issues. In the past we separated the disability and mental health workforce. So we have the opportunity in an accommodation model where people are struggling with mental health issues to put in a mental health worker for some shifts, to provide different expertise.

What are the practical things you're doing to support your team through the extraordinary amount of change you're going through at UCW?

The change is not limited to the workforce. In the leadership team we have a CEO who has been in the role since early 2017. I've been in my role since late 2017 and our Head of Support Services has been in the role since late 2018. But we're all committed to an open-door policy. It's about being available. Previously the organisation was very hierarchical, there was a strong culture of 'permission seeking' and so the move to self-organising teams has to combat that. It's the opposite to: *'Can I do this?'* Instead it's: *'I've done this, so let me know if I should have done it differently.'*

It's not something we can overcome with a few internal seminars and training days. This is something that we have to reinforce in every way we can. We have roadshows, we use the internet hub, and we've eliminated Program Service Managers and now have Practice

Leads who are Subject Matter Experts. We're seeing a new richness of ideas from the cross-pollination of different subject matter experts who are now able to step outside their specific program and explore new opportunities for collaboration – and that's really important and exciting in terms of cultural transformation.

Michael, any final comments?

I believe that we have an obligation to keep the issue of the working poor on the radar for everybody ... for politicians, the NDIA and every provider in the sector.

Chapter 8

Step 5: Create Your Culture Action Plan

'A person who feels appreciated will always do more than what is expected.'

Quinton Douman

Culture is the human side of the business that ensures quality in every process. So a Culture Action Plan is one that recognises that the actual employee experience (not rules, not technology, not compliance) is the key driver of quality customer outcomes.

The Culture Action Plan identifies the actions and tools that create a 'values-driven' employee experience. Throughout this book we've talked about different tools, actions and ideas for building and supporting your workplace culture.

Once you are clear on the key culture stress points (or 'transition points') specific to your workplace you can begin to tailor an effective, measurable Action Plan.

Three uncomfortable truths

To clear the pathways for people to perform at their best, I've found that there are often three uncomfortable truths CEOs need to face.

If these are not addressed then this Action Plan will be a time-consuming exercise that alienates the employees you need to hang onto the most.

None of this is going to work if you are not prepared to:

1. Fire toxic people – even if they are your most productive employees.

2. Address the transition points – really pull them apart, understand them and fix them.

3. Review and (if necessary) reinvent your entire organisational structure. Localise your decision making and only measure what matters.

If this makes you feel uncomfortable, then just acknowledge that your organisation is not ready to drive a Culture Action Plan. However, the longer you delay, the greater your risk of losing great people. Once you begin this process, you will set up expectations that will need to be followed through. If you don't, you still risk losing your smartest people.

Review your organisational structure

It is beyond the scope of this book to dive into the pros and cons of various organisational structures. However, based on the two-pyramid model (see page 49), your frontline employees are the people best placed to understand, support and serve your customer. So it makes sense to decentralise your decision making and tailor your organisational structure to bring you closer to your customer.

For me, the best organisational structure is one that:

• allows every employee to regularly hear the voice of the customer

• delivers measurable value in the eyes of the customer

- enables continuous improvement and incremental innovation based on actual employee and customer feedback

- supports cross-functional teams

- is as flat as you can possibly make it!

As Georgina Chalker – Head of People & Culture at Samaritans Foundation, a NSW-based disability services provider – says in her interview:

> The flatter and leaner you are at a leadership level the more consistent your messaging is at the direct workforce level. What I found working in other organisations that were heavily layered with hierarchical structures is that it really dilutes your ability to spread your cultural message.

disAbility Living, a South Australia–based provider, completely reinvented their entire organisational structure to place their customers at the very top of their structure and their direct support staff the next layer down. Previously a traditional service provider, the organisation successfully transitioned into a customer-focused, values-driven organisation following the same change logic behind the 'two-pyramid' model outlined in chapter 2.[36]

They also created the role of Chief Operating Officer to oversee three departments:

- Client services: responsible for service delivery to clients.

- Community engagement: the first point of contact for clients, regularly checking in on customer satisfaction with services provided, supporting volunteer links and managing all external communications.

- Staff engagement: ensuring values-based recruitment and that all staff are supported on their journey with the organisation. They are there *for the staff*, to support them if and when issues arise.

---

36   disAbility Living's organisational chart is included in 'The Workplace Culture & the NDIS Workbook', available for download from www.fcmarketing.com.au.

'We have turned our structure upside down to put the clients and direct support workers central to everything.'

Anita Bayford, Chief Operating Officer, disAbility Living Inc., SA

How to develop your culture action plan

There are a number of layers you could add to this model thanks to the avalanche of information available around staff engagement. However, from firsthand experience, I've found that the simpler the process, the easier it is to generate immediate incremental 'wins' and the easier it is to create measurable long-term outcomes. It's easier for people to understand it, to share it, to implement it, to test it and to report on it.

When we get to this bit in The Culture Masterclass, I split the group into three teams. The three teams then develop 12-month objectives and strategies for three target markets:

- new staff
- existing staff
- future staff.

The strategies are considered from the point of view of their impact on each market. Each target market can be broken down into segments, but it's easier to start big picture if the team hasn't done this before.

If you are running the process in your own organisation it's also easier to allow people to self-select their preferred team based on where they feel they can most add value.

Why this approach to culture works

I might be repeating stuff here, but it deserves repeating because it's the reason a marketing approach to culture delivers great outcomes.

I group employees into 'target markets' because we need to focus on the employee as an individual with needs, burning issues and problems. Until they feel heard, they won't feel valued. Your strategies and messages need to be framed in the **language** they use and understand, using the **channels** that they use and understand. The better you understand and really get into the head of each of these three target markets, the stronger your Action Plan.

Case study

Sylvanvale Foundation: A crisis of culture starts at the top

Sylvanvale Foundation is a traditional provider of disability services based in southern and western Sydney. Between 2012 and 2015 a series of unsuccessful restructures by two successive CEOs led to a seriously alienated workforce.

There was what Cathy Quinn, Executive Manager of Operations, calls a 'crisis of culture' due to the emerging disconnect between employees' values and Sylvanvale's values.

It seemed as if the organisation had lost touch with its 'why' as both CEOs tried to drive a transformational change agenda through an outdated organisational structure.

They began losing great employees. A staff engagement survey in 2015 found that staff were angry. The increased use of agency staff only led to increased internal friction.

'Sylvanvale has lost its heart ... it has now become very hard nosed ... the attitude seems to be that if you don't like it, leave! ... '

Workforce acquisition was also difficult. A career in disability was rooted in deep stereotypes around the 'carer role', with the focus on 'personal care' versus customer self-actualisation.

'Disability care continues to have a stigma, a negative connotation ... I don't think I could do all that personal needs stuff.'

197

What they did

A strong new values-fit CEO was promoted from within the organisation. She spent 12 months visiting sites, sharing their origin story at every opportunity and increasing her face-to-face visibility with existing staff and clients.

They were honest about the mistakes that had been made and took steps to understand and address the poor internal culture. They understood that co-design was the key to organisational sustainability.

They moved to a localised management structure and frontline site offices became Head Office's customer.

They prioritised existing staff and customers and for 12 months did not actively pursue new clients.

They built in quality, reliability and consistency across their core service streams.

They implemented an internal communications strategy that identified what staff needed to know about costs, processes, services and their own role within Sylvanvale's transition to the NDIS.

They changed the way their recruitment and induction processes, repositioning the role of disability worker as a change-maker.

The four principles

Over the last 24 months I've come to believe there are four key principles for developing an effective, robust Culture Action Plan:

1. All conversations (and strategies) are driven by your specific values. This exercise has to be conducted in a 'safe' space. If this means smaller groups, implement this model over multiple sessions.

2. The strategies are developed collaboratively to secure team ownership and 'buy-in' of the final Action Plan.

3. Little things mean a lot. The employee–customer relationship is at the heart of every strategy. This is about people feeling heard and valued. *This is not about ticking boxes.* This stuff takes time. If you have a mental deadline for 'when everyone will feel great about working here' then you're probably part of the problem.

4. Measure what matters using the SMART framework. (It's **S**pecific **M**easurable **A**chievable **R**ealistic and **T**ime bound.)

Let's have a look at each of these.

1. Conversations and strategies are values based

Your brand values become the starting point for facilitating the team conversations about culture. As mentioned earlier, I refer to them as brand values because they relate directly to your identity – in the eyes of your employees and your customers. These brand values are the glue that holds your culture together and ultimately produces a satisfied customer.

The key is to use your values as the starting point for each brainstorm. The end goal is to tie values to daily actions and behaviours.

For example, if we were truly living the value of *respect*: What's working? What's possible? What do we need to *stop* doing?

Your Action Plan should address the key transition points and reinforce the following relationships for each of the three target markets:[37]

- Connecting employees to the customer. This is the most important relationship of all. It is the reason the organisation exists; it is the reason anyone has a job.

- Connecting the employees to each other.

- Connecting the employees to the organisation and its mission.

---

37 I first came across this distinction in Sybil F. Stershic's book *Share of Mind, Share of Heart: Marketing tools of engagement for nonprofits*, WME Books 2012.

The key relationships in the Culture Action Plan

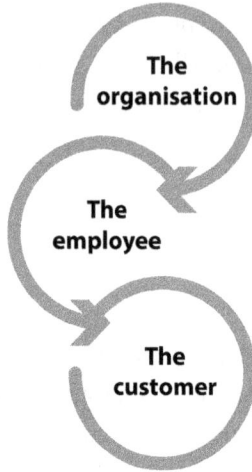

2. Create collaboratively

How you run this model is as important as the content itself. The most effective Action Plans are those developed in collaboration with your staff. They come up with the ideas. This means they identify and prioritise the tools, processes and actions which would make the greatest difference at each transition point and to their overall working environment. If well facilitated, these conversations will unlock great ideas that cost nothing.

This book has already mentioned many of the strategies you could use to populate your plan. Shown below are some examples. Success depends on tailoring it to best suit your needs. (Some strategies appear in more than one column; this indicates a well-integrated plan and means you can generate multiple outcomes from a single strategy.)

Connecting employees to the organisation	Connecting employees to each other	Connecting employees to the customer
A CEO face-to-face strategy. Produce videos: – *My story* – *Why I love my job* – *What we know now about …*	Produce videos: – *My story* – *Why I love my job* – *How I felt when …*	Videos and face-to-face presentations of customers and families: – *How I felt when …* – *My story*
Identify and clarify all roles that are unclear. Review performance measures in each PD. Include measures that are meaningful to your customer and purpose.	Weekly team meetings that begin with a values story and include sharing weekly successes and failures.	Create a 'Living our Brand' handbook linking values to behaviours and explaining 'how we do things around here' and link to our customer promise.
Review your organisational structure, and reduce the layers between your CEO and frontline.	Create a 'Living our Brand' handbook linking values to behaviours and explaining 'how we do things around here' and link to our customer promise.	Create a customer journey map with key personas identified.
Make the Origin Story prominent. Make sure everyone knows how to tell it. Create rewards based on this.	Employee induction and orientation is reviewed with ongoing feedback from recent new team members.	Create scenario exercises/role playing training: what do I do if x? Understand how different teams prefer to learn.
Review how you celebrate personal milestones, how you run meetings, how you train your managers in difficult conversations, etc.	Review how technology can help build culture (e.g. employee profiles via intranet; Slack, Skype or Zoom to connect remote staff)	Develop a consistent buddy system for coaching and training to ensure sufficient individual support.

3. Little things mean a lot

Little things are big things when it comes to creating an authentic culture, because it's the personal, unexpected, thoughtful things that people remember and talk about. For example:

- remembering someone's name or birthday

- celebrating an employee's milestones (new degree? new baby? new role?)

- how you answer the phone: how long you take to answer it, how that makes people feel

- how you greet new employees and make them feel welcome

- how you farewell people: this sends a strong message about what's really going on. For example, do people exit sharing tears and angst with their colleagues, or does someone acknowledge their contribution in front of their team? (If you leave things unsaid, your staff may create their own 'stories' around the departure. Communication vacuums are always filled.)

- surveying your employees and allowing them to say what they think with complete anonymity.

Conversely, big or flashy things can often come across as meaningless and hollow. (I'm thinking corporate-style 'love ins' – those wacky 'team-building exercises' that cost a fortune, take a full day or more, and then you're left wondering who on earth approved this?)

Some examples

A birthday cake can be so much more than a birthday cake

I'll never forget the sense of community I felt when I began working with a fantastic NSW-based advocacy organisation called the Intellectual Disability Rights Service (IDRS). I was hired to prepare a strategic marketing plan for the organisation and was struck by the vibrant sense of cohesiveness across the entire team. Here was a group of people with a strong shared mission and a deep mutual respect for each other.

Funnily enough, it was the simple act of sharing a birthday cake that made this so obvious. I arrived one morning to be invited to join in a birthday celebration. This was no mere token happy birthday song with people dashing back to their desks with their piece of cake on a serviette. This was a full 'everybody-stop-working-because-we-have-a-birthday-today' kind of celebration. Lawyers, clients, student volunteers, legal volunteers, social work volunteers, paralegals, the CEO, the leadership team – everybody in the office was in there singing happy birthday and eating a really fabulous cake. And these were super-busy people, achieving incredible results on a financial shoestring!

IDRS have a fantastic culture and a wonderful sense of humour and community, despite the fact that every day they are supporting people with intellectual disability to get a fair go from the criminal justice system. This means days in court alongside a client, days visiting prisons, days training volunteers, and days when the stories can be heartbreaking.

The 'Three Names' rule

In his *Turn the Ship Around!* workbook, Captain L. David Marquet, Commander of the US Naval submarine the *Santa Fe*, discusses the dilemma of how to change behaviours.[38]

Not all employees will understand what it means to live the values or why this is so important. But Marquet found that when he identified a list of the new observable behaviours that would result from the change in thinking then he could specifically train for it.

The 'Three Name Rule' story is a great example. This rule referred to how you welcomed visitors on board the submarine.

---

38   L. D. Marquet, A. Worshek, *The Turn the Ship Around! Workbook*, Portfolio Penguin 2015.

It was a simple behaviour protocol that immediately changed perceptions and eventually led to a change of thinking:

> **The three name rule consisted of this: when you saw a visitor or inspector on board the *Santa Fe* you would greet them with three names – your name, their name and the name of the submarine: 'Good morning Captain Smith. I am Petty Officer Martinez. Welcome on board the *Santa Fe*.'**

> **The impression was a ship with good morale, but the way we got there wasn't by giving speeches about 'being proud of your ship'. It was giving the crew a tool they could use to actually practice being proud.**

> **The interesting thing was that immediately people visiting the ship noticed and remarked on the difference. As several months passed and more and more of the crew practiced this new behaviour it began to feel more natural ... the words we were repeatedly saying were rewiring our brains so that we actually felt proud of the submarine.**

I love this example because it so resonates with what I see in the disability sector today. So many great employees don't know how to explain what they do or the difference your organisation makes in the lives of the people you serve. Sometimes a simple script that they can tailor is all they need to feel comfortable telling their friends, families and social networks about the great work you do.

Little things mean a lot.

DuPont clarifies 'Respect'

Back in 2011, the multinational organisation DuPont was concerned that one of their brand values lacked clarity. Of their four values – Valuing People, Safety & Health, Ethics and Environmental Stewardship – it was obvious that 'Valuing People' was the least clear and the least trained.

They changed the name of this value to 'Respect for People'. They then ran global training across 70,000 employees to help them understand what this looked like on a daily basis in terms of actual workplace behaviours; to understand what they could measure and why it was important.

This value was revisited every year. They created 'Respect for People' champions who ran workshops at a local level to engage in the topic and embed the language. Every meeting now begins with sharing a story about one of the values in action in the workplace, not just a safety story.[39]

Little things that break a culture: 13 toxic indicators

Little things are also really big things when it comes to cultural 'indicators'. In August 2018 I wrote a post on LinkedIn called '10 Signs Your Workplace Culture May Be Struggling'. The response from some HR professionals really took me by surprise. For some reason, what seemed pretty obvious to me was called 'insightful'.

It's easy to confuse the transactional nature of the 'HR' role with the human side. This is not about putting people into boxes by skill-set. People are not resources of the business; people are the lifeblood of the business. Because what your employees feel, your customers are ultimately going to feel.

From my work over the last 12 months, I've pulled together 13 indicators of a toxic work culture. (You may have more!):

1. Your high performers look disengaged, start arriving late and seem to have lost their passion.

2. There is a focus on processes rather than actually finishing anything (poor project management, lack of accountability).

---

39   For more on DuPont, refer to the case study in 'The Workplace Culture & the NDIS Workbook', available for download from www.fcmarketing.com.au.

3. People struggle with even small decisions and feel threatened by task ownership.

4. Toxic people are entrenched and good people quit.

5. Exit interviews are left uncompleted.

6. Your values are not spoken about regularly and most people can't name them all.

7. Meetings are cancelled without explanation.

8. There are silos of sub-cultures that struggle to communicate effectively with each other.

9. A blurring of the professional boundaries between work life and home life. (For example, staff struggling to prioritise an 'unexpected workload' or supporting customers outside of work hours or in their own homes.)

10. Increased staff turnover and sick days.

11. Excessive reliance on email so people are 'glued' to their inbox.

12. You don't gather and celebrate together anymore because 'things are too busy'.

13. You can't remember hearing laughter.

4. Measure what matters and build feedback loops

We all know that 'what gets measured gets managed', thus the need for smarter measures of culture than just an annual staff engagement survey. But there is a more dynamic, human need for smarter measurement.

High achievers respond to transparent measurement metrics. Your employees have the right to know exactly what great performance looks like in their role and how that will be measured.

'People love to be measured. But measure the right stuff. The right stuff is what creates great performance for customers, the right stuff is what helps you keep learning. The right stuff is what helps you continuously improve.'

Flight of the Buffalo, (1993) JA Belasco and RC Stayer

The final step in the process is one of continuous learning and improvement. It's not enough to create an Action Plan; you need to collect employee and customer feedback at regular intervals (not just your transition points). Because we all own culture, we all have the right to contribute to an improved employee and customer experience. The more personal we can make these feedback loops, the faster your culture will move in the right direction.

Sean Dempsey, CEO of Plan Partners, actually rings every new employee to see how their first day was. He regularly answers incoming customer phone enquiries. This means he hears firsthand how well his business is operating.

The process of creating a great culture

The following diagram outlines my process for creating a great culture in the non-profit workplace. It begins with the fundamentals such as the Vision, the Brand and the Values, and the culture flows from there. In this way, robust, high-performance workplace cultures are modelled and nurtured from the top down and 'owned' by every employee.

Creating a great culture in the non-profit workplace

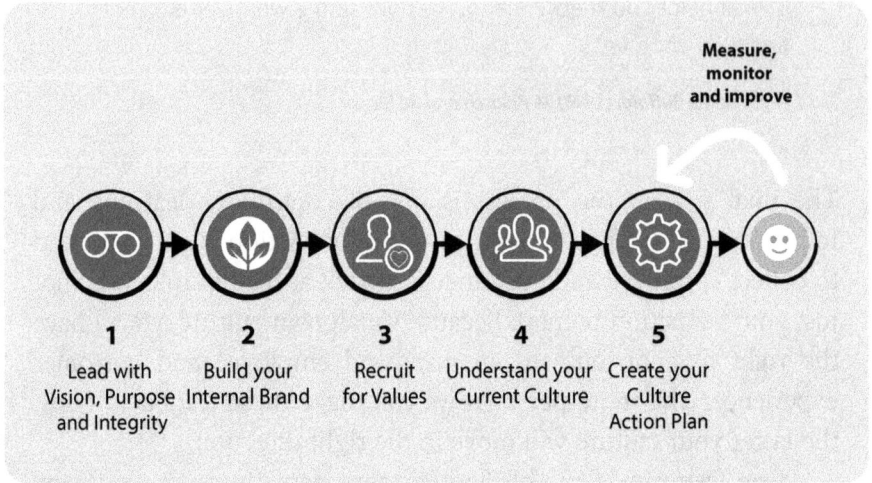

Measure, monitor and improve

1 Lead with Vision, Purpose and Integrity

2 Build your Internal Brand

3 Recruit for Values

4 Understand your Current Culture

5 Create your Culture Action Plan

Summary

▶ The Culture Action Plan identifies the actions and tools that create a values-driven employee experience.

▶ It requires the courage to make tough, uncomfortable decisions.

▶ There are four principles for creating an effective, robust Action Plan.

▶ All conversations and strategies are values based.

▶ The Action Plan is created collaboratively and the process is scaled to suit.

▶ Your strategies address the key transition points.

▶ Strategies are designed to connect employees to the organisation, to each other and to the customer.

▶ Little things are big things when it comes to culture.

▶ Measure what matters and make it SMART.

▶ Ensure continuous feedback loops from the employee and customer experience are implemented to continuously monitor and refine your plan. The more face-to-face the better.

▶ An Action Plan is a document for continuous review.

Interview

Georgina Chalker, Head of People & Culture, Samaritans Foundation

Samaritans provides disability services and care, youth, family, mental health and community support in Newcastle and several regions of NSW. Georgina Chalker is responsible for Samaritan's workforce management and employee experience.

With a background in mining and manufacturing, she has spent the last three-plus years within the community services sector focused on building high-performing teams. Georgina has designed a dynamic model for delivering services with three fundamental tenets: customer satisfaction, partnership and continuous improvement.

What do you think are the biggest challenges facing the community services sector right now?

I think the greatest challenge is the lag we have had in the development of best practice workforce management and inadequate recognition of how intricately connected employee engagement and customer experience truly are. Previously those strategies and concepts were quite separate, if they existed at all. Now we're seeing the challenges of attracting and retaining staff and there is better appreciation that the value measurement equation depends on our employees because direct support and meaningful relationships with Support Workers are unequivocally what customers value most. It is why they come to us and why they come back.

It's almost like going back and trying to catch up because it just wasn't the industry's focus before. The focus was very much risk and compliance. In many organisations, there has been an emphasis on clinical innovation and governance but a lack of investment in core workforce fundamentals.

Workforce planning is still relatively immature considering the nature of what we do and, in the absence of strong leadership, even at a strategic level the primary workforce framework can be lost among other aspirational goals. Knowing that the employee group is really the core asset of the organisation, it's so foreign to think that it could ever be omitted from that strategic piece.

From the recent data, it's pretty clear that the disability sector and the aged-care sector will be competing for the same, very small workforce pool. If you had one key message for providers in disability and aged care right now what would it be?

To design workforce strategies that genuinely value the direct support that is delivered at the customer level. To start to think about the Support Worker role as a career, as a genuine profession, and invest heavily in talent management. We need to shift away from an exclusive emphasis on prescriptive, competency-based training to look at a person's potential and how we enliven that. There needs to be defined progression pathways and development opportunities that motivate and engage. I don't think that we are going to be able to fulfil the talent attraction/retention piece until we get that right.

You made a key point earlier around measuring performance in terms of the customer's own individual experience of a staff member. How do you actually do that in practice?

The service provision of the direct workforce is the most critical component for customer satisfaction and positive health and well-being outcomes. This is the 'make or break' success factor. Build customer experience data points that validate why we are investing in our primary workforce, evidence that it is a major driver of customer outcomes, retention and growth. Capitalise on the opportunity to feed information about impact back to staff. Staff often *feel* their importance when they are with the customer but they don't see the organisation recognising and rewarding them so they feel disconnected; you have to bring staff together by uniting a sense of shared purpose.

So how do you collect those data points?

A customer advocacy function is my preferred method. This means proactively contacting customers through surveys and championing the customer engagement process at all levels. It also means catching all of the ways customer feedback can come to you and setting a clear process around what your staff do with that information.

Part of this is making people feel comfortable with reporting direct feedback. They need to understand that they are not boasting and that direct feedback helps us improve our service and recognise performance. This means inviting staff as well as customer feedback.

A customer advocacy function that includes formal and informal feedback management is really important because that data informs continuous improvement and assists to identify your strengths and weaknesses.

You have to acknowledge your team when they demonstrate their commitment to excellence, visibly and vocally, to reinforce what you value and why you value it. Each team member needs to understand how they contribute to positive customer outcomes; the measurement of key indicators enables success to be clearly communicated and this unites and engages teams. This sparks the buy in that an organisation needs to genuinely make a difference.

How do you address the issue of attracting future staff? Do you necessarily look for industry experience? What do you feel is best practice?

It requires evolving to a more flexible service framework. In terms of service delivery, look at what is most important for customer engagement: building rapport and relationships and target candidates that demonstrate skills and enthusiasm in these areas. It's about *how* you are delivering something not just what you deliver.

Accompanying that is a whole range of different attributes that you seek in a candidate. I think it really expands the pool of people you might want in your organisation. In the hospitality and retail sectors, the expectation is that if you don't deliver something great the person won't be back.

Customer service orientation must be a primary selection driver. The desire to serve is either within you or it is not. Once you have identified that intrinsic motivator, everything else is trainable. I think you can train all day long, every day, and if you don't have that piece you will never achieve an exceptional customer experience; you will always be teetering on mediocre to average.

What role does culture play at Samaritans? How do you see it improving, adding value to the organisation?

Culture for me is everything. It's the ultimate measure because it speaks to values. It becomes rhetoric if your leadership team are not living or breathing it in every interaction. The customer's interests must be at the centre of every decision. People will see from the leadership modelling whether that culture rings true. If it's not genuine they will call out the lack of credibility and you won't get that powerful team alignment.

One of the things that attracted me to Samaritans is the strength of our culture. It is so palpable, honest and genuine. The real benefit coming into this role was that the cultural foundation was already there. It is a solid platform that allows us to build an elevated organisational vision where everybody is striving to achieve the same goals.

In organisations where the culture is weak you're really only ever repairing. You are continually going back and fixing things. You get stuck in that cycle of 'band-aiding'. You can't ever achieve the synergy that's possible when you have cultural cohesion across your teams. A highly engaged team will contribute discretionary effort and the combined effect of that across a large group is that you lift your organisational capacity and performance significantly without any additional cost.

What would be your advice to a disability provider working with a legacy model? Their staff are undergoing severe change fatigue and are possibly confronted by the mission versus market. How would you approach a gig like that?

When I first started in the aged-care sector there was a lot of resistance to change and a sense that the sector was being commercialised. I think the way to turn that around is to take the passion that people have, their natural energy, their desire to contribute, and then attach that to a purpose which isn't about sustainability, which isn't about profit – it's actually about a customer receiving a service. It is as simple and as complicated as that. At the end of the day, every process, function and framework is focused towards that ultimate outcome, and that is why people work in this sector so that is what you need to appeal to in order to capture their hearts and minds.

How has the organisational structure of Samaritans changed and does that support your culture?

The flatter and leaner you are at a leadership level the more consistent your messaging is at the direct workforce level. What I found working in other organisations that were heavily layered with hierarchical structures is that it really dilutes your ability to spread your cultural message. You get multiple interpretations of your message along the way; you may encounter disgruntled managers and then the link is broken in terms of culture.

We have a flat, lean structure at Samaritans. I am directly connected to our workforce and I can access what is happening in real time. You don't have to wait for a major issue or problem to arise because you are always 'in' your operation – learning, understanding and making incremental changes before massive cracks appear.

I believe we need to see the customer experience and the employee experience as the two sides of the one relationship. It follows then that continuity of frontline staff is central to delivering a quality customer and employee experience. How do you overcome the issues of continuity of care?

This is a project that we have worked on at Samaritans. It is baffling in a way when you think of it logically. The customer is seeking continuity of care, a reliable rotating core group of workers. An employee is seeking pretty much the same thing, and yet we are in a workforce that is heavily casualised – the antithesis of reliability and continuity.

Employment status is 101. It is the first fundamental. How do I demonstrate my loyalty, my investment in an individual if I can't even offer you a permanent contract that says: *'We are committed, I believe in you, in what you bring to the organisation, I want you to stay with us for a long time'?*

We are in the process of setting our workforce up so that we have the vast majority of staff as permanent part time, and then we use our casual workforce as genuinely supplementary, not as quasi permanent without any of the safety on either side for employee or customer.

It is seriously detrimental to positive customer outcomes to maintain a transient casual workforce; employee turnover is a huge unrecoverable cost that warrants an organisation's full attention. Look at simple financial measures like induction cost and return on your training investment; the numbers will be compelling. We have to start doing things differently if we are going to be sustainable in the future; that is the burden and the privilege of working in community services during a time of change.

I'm particularly interested in how you induct and support new team members at Samaritans and whether you have additional layers of support in that first three months. Do you run buddy systems? How do you ensure that people feel heard and supported?

One of the challenges with new staff is that there are certain things that you won't share with your manager when you are new to a role. There is a greater readiness to engage with someone who is a peer. It's really critical, especially for people who have not worked in community services before. It requires such high autonomy to go into a home by yourself; the pressure in terms of decision making is high, and if you don't have someone to debrief with then it can become a really challenging role.

Chapter 9 ▶▶

What now?

'I'm a success today because I had a friend who believed in me and I didn't have the heart to let him down.'

Abraham Lincoln

So much has already been written about organisational culture. I hope that you have found some fresh insights and the practical, takeaway value you were looking for. (I'd love to hear your feedback! If you have time, please drop me a line: fran@fcmarketing. com.au.)

As I write these words, the NDIS is once again in the media. This week, four senior NDIA staff have resigned in the wake of the last CEO, so I've just updated chapter 1 – again.

The NDIS is a visionary reform that was conceived by big-thinking people. Yet the calibre of that thinking either has not translated into its implementation, or, if it has, it's been undermined by political constraints, despite the best intentions of the thousands of well-meaning people involved.

The funding model is a blunt instrument that has been emasculated by rushed participant targets and bureaucratic processes.

From a marketer's viewpoint, we need to be a lot smarter about how it is modified to suit different market segments (for example, rural and regional communities, non-English speaking communities, indigenous communities).

From a human rights viewpoint, we need to urgently address how this model interfaces with other government agencies and services, so that *nobody is worse off* as a result of the NDIS. (The recent COAG reforms are an overdue but welcome step in the right direction.)

Last week, during a work trip to the mining town of Moranbah in central Queensland, I heard stories of market failure. These stories involved people considered not eligible for the NDIS. These were people with multiple sclerosis, mental health issues and other problems: 40 people who previously relied on 10 to 15 hours a week of support will now only receive one hour of support, and 16 people now have no services at all.

Your customers deserve a smarter NDIS that provides the choice, quality and opportunity they were promised to lead a 'normal life' – regardless of their disability, ethnicity or postcode. If we can modify this funding model so that it could be *flexible in the face of the different needs* of the communities it is intended to serve, then there is hope.

Your employees also deserve the opportunity to earn a decent living from a fair roster in a workplace where they feel safe, valued and supported.

Writing this book and interviewing the generous thought leaders and CEOs has again been a very humbling experience. There is so much talent, goodwill, passion and experience in the Australian disability sector! I am indebted to every disability support worker and every manager who trusted me to respect their confidentiality whenever they asked me to. This book would be much poorer without their input.

Be a champion for your employees

It is my belief that when you commit to creating a better organisational culture, you're committing to being a champion, not just for your customers but also for your employees.

So I'd like to ask you to share more. Share your successes and your failures, your great NDIS stories and your horror stories. So that we can all learn what's working, what isn't working and what's possible.

If it feels right, please also share this book with your staff. Let them discuss how they would like to drive their culture program and get back to you with their suggestions and recommendations. Everybody owns culture. It's a top-down, inside-out, never-ending process that begins with integrity of leadership.

Acknowledgements

Four years ago now, I said to my family, 'Okay, whatever happens, *don't ever let me write another book!'*

At the time, I was thinking that the weeks without weekends, the RSI, and more particularly, the time I could have spent with my mum (she died the day after my first book was released) was unlikely to have been worth it.

But … that first book is now in its seventh reprint and I am still blown away by the generosity of people who bought first editions and second editions and still came back for repeat orders and those who sent lovely feedback. Now I know mum would be proud.

Grateful is still the only word that comes to mind as I write this second acknowledgement. It still looks like too small a word to adequately describe how I feel right now. Writing a book is a team sport. And once again, I was lucky enough to have fantastic players on my team.

This book would not have been possible without the CEOs and thought leaders who gave so generously of their time, support and insights during our interviews: Rob White, Elise Taylor and Frank Sedmack from Cerebral Palsy Alliance, Laura O'Reilly from Fighting Chance, David Moody from National Disability Services, Kerry Stubbs from Northcott, Nicola Hayhoe from The Housing Connection, Aviva Beecher from Clickability, Robyn Kaczmarek from The Co-operative Life, Michael Chester from UnitingCare West, Georgina Chalker from Samaritans Foundation, Leanne Fretten from Sylvanvale Foundation, Melinda Kubisa from Community Living Options, Sean Dempsey from Plan Partners and Anita Bayford from disAbility Living Inc.

I'd also like to thank my behind-the-scenes team of professionals who supported me every step of the way: Michael Hanrahan and Anna Clemann from Michael Hanrahan Publishing, Eimer Boyle, Dianne Masri, Andrew Griffiths, Amanda Hickey and Roxanne Walker.

Nobody understands the NDIS pricing model and the impacts it has had on the Australian disability sector better than Professor David J. Gilchrist. I'm proud to include him in this book and grateful that he agreed to write the Foreword.

A huge thank you to the people with disability, their families, frontline support workers and managers who trusted me with their stories, frustrations and dreams. This book would not have happened without you.

You learn a lot of things writing 60,000-plus words. This time around, I learnt how hard it is to write when you're also running a busy small business. So the award for 'Most Patient Family Members on the Planet' goes to my husband Paul and daughter Sophie. I will always be grateful for the gift of you both in my life.

ALSO BY FRAN CONNELLEY

If you've enjoyed reading this book then you may find these other titles by Fran Connelley of interest.

The Workplace Culture and The NDIS Workbook
Create a high performance culture in your organisation.

The Workplace Culture and the NDIS Workbook is the online companion workbook to this book. In it you will find practical exercises, videos, discussion guides, organisational charts and more practical tools to help you apply her methods in your organisation.

Additional materials include resources developed by Cerebral Palsy Alliance, Plan Partners, Sylvanvale Foundation, The Cooperative Life and more.

Whether you work for a city-based non-profit or within a network of remote self-managed teams, this workbook is designed to help you create a vibrant, connected, mission-driven culture in your organisation.

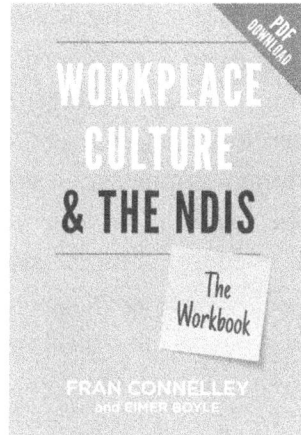

Download the interactive PDF file directly from
www.fcmarketing.com.au

How To Thrive Under The NDIS: A pathway to sustainability

The Australian disability sector is currently undergoing massive macro and micro changes. The National Disability Insurance Scheme is the most significant market disrupter this sector has ever experienced.

How to Thrive Under the NDIS was written in 2015 for CEOs of disability organisations seeking to achieve financial sustainability and deliver innovative, best-practice services that meet the needs of people with disabilities. It includes Fran's Seven Steps to Sustainability and interviews with CEOs and thought leaders from Australia and the UK. This bestseller also covers the critical strategic issues to be resolved: understanding your customer and your market, knowing exactly where you excel, owning your niche and identifying strategic 'mission-fit' partners.

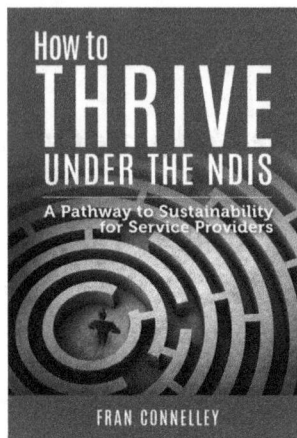

'This book is my NDIS marketing bible.'

Kylie Johnson, Senior Media & Communications Adviser – Australian Red Cross

'This book is a breath of fresh air. It is helping me in my leadership of Melbourne City Mission get all parts of the organisation on board. It is easy to navigate, logical and educative!'

Liz Bishop, CEO interim, Melbourne City Mission

Available from www.fcmarketing.com.au, Amazon and Booktopia

WORKSHOP PROGRAMS

There are several programs available to help you implement Fran's methodology and bring your brand alive. To check availability or find out more email fran@fcmarketing.com.au.

The 'Bringing The Brand Alive' workshop program

Imagine if every employee in your organisation felt that they personally 'owned' your brand. The *'Bringing the Brand Alive'* Program provides the missing piece of work between the Brand and the internal team ownership of the Brand to create a customer-focused, brand-driven, high-performance culture. Facilitated by Fran Connelley, this workshop program is delivered as in-house training, fully customised to each organisation. The key deliverable is a 12-month Culture Action Plan. The program is spread over four to six weeks and follows a proven 5-step methodology.

'We collaborated to create a "real" Action Plan with values-based, culture-driven content. I'd rate it 10/10.'

Mel Kubisa, CEO, Community Living Options

'Fran Connelley has challenged the disability industry to think differently about our customers and position them in the centre of everything we do. She has given our organisation the confidence to stick to our guns during a time when glossy rebrands were the norm and focus on supporting our staff through one of the biggest culture change processes of our organisation's history. If Fran says it, do it.'

Jess Brown, Group Manager, Business Growth, Marathon Health

The Culture Masterclass

The Culture Masterclass is an intensive one-day 'train-the-trainer' version of the Bringing The Brand Alive Program that provides managers with the practical skills and tools to run an effective culture program in their own organisation. Facilitated by Fran Connelley, this workshop covers the key exercises from her highly successful, fully customised program.

> **'Fran's Culture Masterclass was one of the best workshops I've ever attended and one that I will measure all future workshops against. Loved it! The activities were fabulous! 10/10.'**
>
> *Mandy Zankar, HR Director, Vivid Vic*

The Strategic Marketing Program

The Strategic Marketing Program was created for any non-profit organisation facing a withdrawal of government 'block' funding and a highly competitive, customer-centric marketplace. The content is fully customised to each organisation and results in a 12-month Brand Strategy and Action Plan.

Using a proven 4-step process, Fran takes a 'whole-of-organisation' approach to the marketing function. She builds on the work you may have already done to develop a lean, targeted and fully functional Action Plan. Over the last few years she has conducted this program for small providers and large $100-million-plus organisations seeking to identify their unique value proposition, consolidate their marketing strategy and use their brand to drive strategic growth.

> **'Working with Fran wasn't like working with other consultants. We came away excited about the future and confident about the path we want to follow. Can't recommend her more highly.'**
>
> *Philip Petrie, CEO, Allevia*

Speaker

If you're looking for a speaker who will inspire and educate your audience with memorable stories and impactful frameworks, Fran regularly presents to community groups, organisations and boards on practical ways to address the changing disability landscape. When it comes to non-profit marketing and workplace culture she speaks with absolute authenticity and authority, drawing on actual case studies.

> 'Fran has a natural ability to connect emotionally and effectively to motivate and inspire both a community and corporate audience. She understands the external policy and social landscape and can subsequently tailor her communication style to a diverse audience.'
>
> *Simone Power, Engagement & Partnerships Manager, Cerebral Palsy Support Network*

1-to-1 Coaching

The NDIS landscape requires leaders to develop new skills without the funding or time to do so. Fran's coaching packages provide affordable, targeted support on a flexible, remote basis. She works with CEOs and managers seeking a confidential sounding board. Each session is 60 minutes via Zoom video call or phone. Availability is limited.

Free stuff

Watch free training videos or sign up for Fran's blog at www.fcmarketing.com.au.

www.ingramcontent.com/pod-product-compliance
Lightning Source LLC
Chambersburg PA
CBHW071158210326
41597CB00016B/1591